WHAT THE THREE MAIN PARTIES
ARE NOT TELLING YOU

Published under licence 2015 by Searching Finance Ltd.

ISBN: 978-1-907720-13-0

Typeset and designed by Deirdré Gyenes

WHAT THE THREE MAIN PARTIES ARE NOT TELLING YOU

A radical way out of stagnation and inequality

Edited by
Michael Meacher

Searching finance

About the author

Michael Meacher was a member of Labour's NEC and Shadow Cabinet in the 1980-90s and Minister for the Environment 1997-2003. His latest book 'The State We Need: Keys to the Renaissance of Britain' was recently published.

About Searching Finance

Searching Finance publishes on economics, finance, politics and history. For more information visit http://www.searchingfinance.com.

CONTENTS

FOREWORD

By Michael Meacher

THE DRIVING FORCE behind this set of contributions on the general theme of a way out of endless austerity and ballooning inequality is the urgency of demonstrating that such a path is necessary, practical and affordable when all the political parties in the UK, and with few exceptions across the Eurozone too, are arguing that there is no alternative to continuing spending cuts into the indefinite future. This has now become the key issue in the Western world, the central canard of our times, and as evidence of secular stagnation grows ever wider, it is high time that this totemic error is challenged and if found grievously wanting, replaced.

The contributors, all well-known and expert in their various fields, offer a range of different dimensions which comprehensively analyse this issue and present both a theoretical and practical alternative to the governing neoliberal ideology. If these ideas and proposals were adopted, they would transform the political landscape across Western economies.

The book opens with the reproduction of an article written in 2011 by David Blanchflower which is designed to show the arguments prevailing in the early stages of this long-drawn-out crisis. The extraordinary fantasy of expansionary fiscal

1

contraction took a grip with Osborne's chancellorship, though it had been convincingly refuted by similar historical experiments in 1923 and 1931. The chimera was promoted further by ignoring the role of the public sector in the rescue after the 2008–09 crash, by ill-judged comparisons of the UK economy with Greece, and by vain expectations of a manufacturing-led recovery when nothing had been done to rebalance an economy lopsidedly over-weighted towards the finance sector. Blanchflower emphasises a medium-term plan for the deficit and a short-term plan to boost growth driven by tax cuts to firms focused on job creation, especially for the young.

Michael Burke stresses the strike of private investment as key both to the cause of the crisis and to the continued delay in recovery. He pinpoints this strike as responsible for the renewed widening of the trade gap, the snail's pace of reducing the government deficit, and the growth of menial and low-paid jobs. He also takes issue with the view that all that is required for recovery is increased demand, since both household and government consumption have increased, but crucially, investment has not. Of the total fall in investment since the recession began, about half is attributable to private firms, while some 10% derives from government. He argues that in the face of the continuing strike by private investors and the failure of the banks to lend to industry on the scale required, there is now a critical need for public investment to kick-start the economy on the route to sustainable growth.

In a forensic examination of the official Office for National Statistics (ONS) Quarterly National Accounts John Mills takes apart the conventional wisdom, firstly, that austerity is the right and necessary means to reduce the government deficit and, secondly, that it is supposed to be doing so, when in fact it isn't. He convincingly demonstrates that with the balance of payments deficit spiralling upwards to probably £80bn this year, in addition to net borrowing by consumers limited by still falling wages and business investment remaining flat (on strike), the government deficit – the balancing item – can hardly reduce and may well get higher.

Pursuing this analysis further, my own contribution to this book argues that, while Alastair Darling's two expansionary budgets in 2009–10 reduced the deficit by nearly £40bn within two years, Osborne's austerity budgets slowed the reduction to a trickle till in 2014 it is likely to go back up again to over £100bn. I argue that the Conservatives are nevertheless continuing to turn the screws of austerity, because for them this is a once-in-a-lifetime heaven-sent opportunity to complete the Thatcher counter-revolution by shrinking the state and squeezing the welfare state into a fully marketised capitalist system. As the alternative way to cut the deficit, I promulgate a major programme of public investment to kick-start the economy into sustainable growth, job creation and rising wages, funded with no increase in public borrowing at all, by instructing the publicly owned banks RBS and Lloyds to prioritise investment in British industry, or by a modest further tranche of quantitative easing (printing money) targeted not at the banks but directly at manufacturing, or by taxation of the 1% ultra-rich.

Mariana Mazzucato adds to this picture by powerfully refuting the conventional idea that the role of the state is simply to redress market failures by showing how the state has a much wider and far more important role by funding not only the rate of innovation, but also envisioning its direction. She shows how the entrepreneurial state, in dozens of examples she cites across the world, is willing and able to take on the early capital-intensive risk areas which the private sector tends to fear. She argues that, in order to promote transformation of the economy by creating and shaping technologies, sectors and markets, the state must organise itself so that it has the 'intelligence' (policy capacity) to think big and formulate bold policies. This opens up a profound re-evaluation of the relationship between state and markets, not in adversarial or subordinate terms, but in terms of public policy setting the direction and route of change by shaping and creating markets, rather than just fixing them.

Now that there are clear signs that Osborne's so-called recovery is already fading and he largely blames the eurozone for the weakness of the UK economy, it is instructive to analyse what function the eurozone really plays in the European economy. Costas Lapavitsas describes its conservative architecture, both in disallowing systematic fiscal transfers and therefore preventing the mutualisation of the public debt of member countries, and also in creating a central bank that focuses entirely on price stability without including other targets such as high levels of employment and economic activity. He shows how this entrenches competitive advantage for Germany whilst at the same time dealing with shocks and disequilibria through lower wages and higher unemployment in other member countries. Even Germany itself faces recession in 2015 as its exports strategy falls short and weak domestic demand drags the economy down, exactly as Osborne's policies currently inflict on the UK.

Returning to the new role for public ownership, Kelvin Hopkins surveys its history from the post-war social democratic consensus, through the Thatcher launch of privatisation as a counter-ideology and the continued neoliberal programme under New Labour, to the growing disenchantment with market fundamentalism after the 2008–09 financial and economic collapse. He then advocates the restoration of public ownership (though not of the Morrisonian bureaucratic ilk), not only in areas where privatisation has proved egregiously greedy and expensive and provided poor service and low investment such as rail, water and energy, but in other areas of manifest market failures, including housing, pensions, banking and PFI.

On the same tack, Ha-Joon Chang notes that the tide of popular opinion is slowly moving against privatisation and in favour of renewed public control, with polled majorities so large (70–80%) that they clearly include large numbers of Conservatives and members of other political parties. He cites among many other international examples: Singapore, known for its free trade policy and welcome for foreign investments, which nevertheless has state-owned enterprises producing 22% of its national output, not just the 'usual suspects' of airline, telecommunications and electricity, but also semi-conductors, engineering and shipping. He also quotes Taiwan as another east Asian miracle economy with a very large state-run sector, and Brazil's public sector that includes the world's third largest civilian aircraft manufacturer as well as Petrobras, the world leader in deep-sea drilling. But above all, he cites the US military as the most successful state enterprise in human history, which has almost single-handedly established the modern information economy.

But it's not only neoliberal ideology which urgently needs replacing, it's also the deeply dysfunctional banking network. Prem Sikka spells out in detail the extraordinary but little understood record of the Big 4 banks in terms of speculative gambling and corruption, above all in toxic derivatives which continue to pose a very dangerous risk, which six years after the crash, has not been remedied. Whilst the casino mentality pervades investment banking, he draws attention to the string of scandals that has also infected retail banking. He then proposes the most systematic set of reforms yet produced, 29 proposed measures in all, which would then radically transform banking into what it is meant to do – serve British industry and the national interest.

Since the exit from recession cannot be a return to business-as-usual, as the descent into secular stagnation is slowly proving, it requires a new architecture. Globalisation, deregulation of finance, untrammelled markets, privatisation, and suppression of the trade unions have not only led to the biggest global crash for nearly a century, they have also generated in the last three decades a poorer economic record in almost every respect than the managed markets regime of the previous three decades. A very different ideology is now urgently required. One element of that must be an enhanced role for the trade unions as partners in economic decision-making, together with the revival of collective bargaining, the coverage of which has precipitously fallen from 82% of workers in 1979 to 23% today. Len McCluskey sets out how this should be achieved and how that would play a significant part in countering the grossly excessive inequality which disfigures Britain today.

The politics of the new ideology are set out in sharp and clear terms by Austin Mitchell. A fundamental new approach is needed which he sets out in a 10-point list of reforms. That includes economic demand management which has been scandalously neglected in recent years, an industrial policy which Britain almost uniquely still lacks, rebalancing the economy from finance to production which is constantly talked about but never done, a competitive exchange rate favouring manufacturing rather than the City, a tax system that encourages building long-term market share rather than short-term profiteering and artificial tax avoidance, and genuine devolution of power both to regions and local authorities.

A key question of any major economic and social programme is how it is to be funded. Richard Murphy tackles the tax gap which has dramatically grown in recent years because of the increasingly extensive use of tax havens by multinational corporations and the super-rich. He explains how the gap may amount to a loss to the Exchequer each year of as much as £120bn, made up of tax evaded (which he believes may total nearly four times the estimate made by HMRC), tax avoided (not illegal, but certainly anti-social), and tax written off as a bad debt or debt discharged by the tax authorities. He then proposes a set of reforms, which for the first time would hugely limit the gross excesses of inequality which even the IMF is now declaring have gone too far. That includes country-by-country reporting for multinationals, abolition of the domicile rule, a comprehensive general anti-avoidance rule in UK law, and a big increase in the HMRC tax inspectorate to tackle tax evasion, especially via private limited companies.

A fairer tax system, an extension of collective bargaining and an economic policy prioritising a return to full employment should greatly reduce inequality. Richard Wilkinson & Kate Pickett show how today's huge income differences damage the well-being, not just of the poor, but of the vast majority of the population, and how this reflects not just material variations but also psycho-social evaluations in an increasingly distrusting and stressed society. They believe that if the disadvantages produced by the unhealthy outcomes spelt out in 'The Spirit Level' are to be avoided, inequality needs to be halved in British society. This would require long-term change – not just tax adjustments at the top of the income scale, but embedding greater equality into the structure of society by increasing democratic accountability within companies, encouraging more mutuals or employee-owned companies, and incentivising measures that promote community life which increases trust between each other.

Another aspect of quality of life is sustainability. In a scathing essay, Alan Simpson vigorously rails against the missed opportunities of the energy revolution and presents a picture of the huge changes now taking place in renewable/decentralised energy systems elsewhere (particularly in Denmark and Germany) compared with the UK still clinging to 'old energy' fossil fuel power. He shows how the German transformation programme (Energiewende) required no government subsidy, generated hundreds of thousands of new jobs, made huge savings in avoided fuel imports, and made a big annual increase to GDP. For Britain he argues for a set of visionary commitments, including energy efficiency to take half a million households a year out of fuel poverty, community-owned renewable energy generation giving priority grid access to renewables, futures markets that sell energy saving as much as energy consumption, and new interconnectors as part of a UK strategic reserve.

Yet another perquisite for a good society is high-quality affordable housing. Austin Mitchell spells out the ignominious story whereby after 18 years of Thatcher-Major's disinvestment which privatised much of the social housing stock, New Labour reduced social and council housing build to a trickle, and then the current Conservative government halved capital funding for social housing, raised rents to an often unaffordable 80% of market rates, and introduced fixed term tenancies and means-testing which turned secure tenancies into over-priced transit camps. To counter this desolation, he advocates a big programme of public housing build (at least a quarter of a million a year) funded either by local authority housing bonds underwritten by the Treasury, or by pension funds or QE. Housing Revenue Accounts and Right to Buy sales should remain the council's own money for housing, not be siphoned off as a Treasury milch cow. Rents should be set by councils geared to local housing need, and the public housing stock should be run with the full involvement and co-operation of the tenants.

Perhaps the last and most important ingredient of quality of life is a sustainable lifestyle. Caroline Lucas shows how the equality and security concerns of the 1930s have been pushed aside in the post-1945 world by consumerism and obsession with GDP growth at all costs. Yet the consequences – GDP a poor indicator of quality of life, Galbraith's 'private wealth and public squalor', and an accelerated boom and bust capitalist cycle – together with the over-exploitation of the natural world and the growing threat of climate change pose powerful warnings signs that the model is no longer sustainable. She posits instead not merely redesigning industrial processes to be more efficient and less polluting, but more profoundly, replacing the false god of GDP with a new shared goal – a commitment to equality and security throughout society which can turn the environmental imperative into a potent agent for social and economic renewal.

I believe this set of essays collectively opens up a new vision out of the tired and sterile arguments that have crippled politics over the last decade or more and points, not just to a radical way out of stagnation and inequality, but to a more profound transformation of our society that so many of our people long for. I hope our readers will agree with that verdict too.

CHAPTER 1

A GROWTH AND JOBS STRATEGY AS THE ALTERNATIVE TO THE CUTS

By David Blanchflower

David Blanchflower is Professor of Economics at Dartmouth College, New Hampshire, Economics Editor of the New Statesman, and former member of the Bank of England's Monetary Policy Committee

ON THE 6ᵀᴴ OCTOBER members of the Monetary Policy Committee at the Bank of England voted unanimously for an additional £75 billion of quantitative easing (QE) because the UK economy is slowing fast. Most economists polled beforehand did not expect the MPC to move so soon and those that did thought they would do only £50 billion. Central banks generally don't pull surprises, so the fact they moved unexpectedly with larger amounts than the markets were expecting implies the economic outlook is far from good. The statement that was released on the day of the decision was especially scary.

"Vulnerabilities associated with the indebtedness of some euro-area sovereigns and banks have resulted in severe strains in bank funding markets and financial markets more generally. These tensions in the world economy threaten the UK recovery."

As a past member of the MPC I know how important the choice of words is as precedent in central bank communications is taken extremely seriously. The nine members would have been well aware that using the word "threaten," which they would not have used lightly, and which they had never used before in any communications, would make the markets think they had seen something the rest of us hadn't seen. In all likelihood they had – and there was zero chance it was good news. Various members of the MPC including the Governor have subsequently made it clear that there is probably a lot more QE to come, as it appears the UK is headed back into recession.

I am afraid none of this comes as much of a surprise to me as I have warned this would happen these many months. At the outset I was opposed to the coalition's austerity programme, which was driven by an ideological hatred of the state and had little connection with the facts. George Osborne apparently believed in a fairy story, which involved an *expansionary fiscal contraction,* where cuts in public spending miraculously lead to a resurgence of the private sector despite the fact that there was no historical precedent in any country to suggest that such an approach would work. The newly formed Office of Budget Responsibility wrongly went along with that illusion, claiming that unemployment would fall and output would rise in every year of this parliament.

Embarrassingly for Osborne, at the time of the Autumn statement, the OBR is going to revise down its overly optimistic forecast for growth and employment once again, and by a lot, when it produces new estimates in November 2011. The reality is that it was always going to lead to a *contractionary fiscal contraction,* which is what has now occurred and unsurprisingly output has collapsed. Output fell by 7.4% between Q2 2008 to Q2 2009 and subsequently recovered 2.8% through Q3 2010 under Alistair Darling, who successfully lifted the

UK economy out of recession. Between Q4 2010 and Q2 2011, GDP growth was zero and there is every prospect that the UK economy is headed back into recession.

One uncomfortable fact that Osborne ignored was that during 2007 and 2008 it was the private sector that failed and it was the public sector that came to its rescue – Northern Rock, RBS and Lloyds only survived because Gordon Brown and Alistair Darling saved them. On day one they should have announced a plan for growth; after 17 months in office and many years in opposition they still don't have one.

I suspect one of the biggest mistakes the Coalition has made has been to talk down the economy, which has now come back to haunt them. Osborne, Cameron and Clegg in particular, described the UK as 'bankrupt' when it never has been in our lifetimes which destroyed business and consumer confidence. Bond yields were low under the Labour government and didn't move at all when there was talk of a LibDem/Labour coalition. They are currently low, as they are in every country with its own central bank and currency, because markets see no prospect of interest rates rising due to the economy's dreadful growth prospects under current policies.

Osborne and Cameron have regularly compared the UK to Greece and latterly to Italy. These countries are stuck in monetary union, do not have their own central bank and are unable to depreciate their currency. Interestingly, in October the United Nations published its 2011 rankings for the ease of doing business (www.doingbusiness.org/rankings). The UK ranked seventh, while Italy ranked 87th and Greece 100th, narrowly beaten out by Yemen in 99th place and Vietnam in 98th. Talking down the economy appears to have been done for political gain but has had the unintended consequence of scaring the consumer away even before the misguided cuts to public services hit home.

The chart overleaf presents evidence on consumer and business confidence based on data from the European Commission that are collected monthly in comparable form in every EU member country. Data are presented for four business groups – manufacturing; services; retail and construction, along with a consumer confidence indicator. Keynes' *animal spirits* dropped sharply in all sectors between 2007 and the beginning of 2009. Confidence picked up fast as monetary and fiscal policy were loosened in 2009 but have subsequently fallen back and are now at levels seen in the depths of recession in 2008. Consumer confidence took another big jump downwards in October 2011, confirming the findings of other surveys including Markit's Household Finance Index, which showed that public sector workers are especially downbeat about their future household incomes. Of particular concern is that declines in confidence in 2007 were good predictors of drops in output and the rise in unemployment that followed.

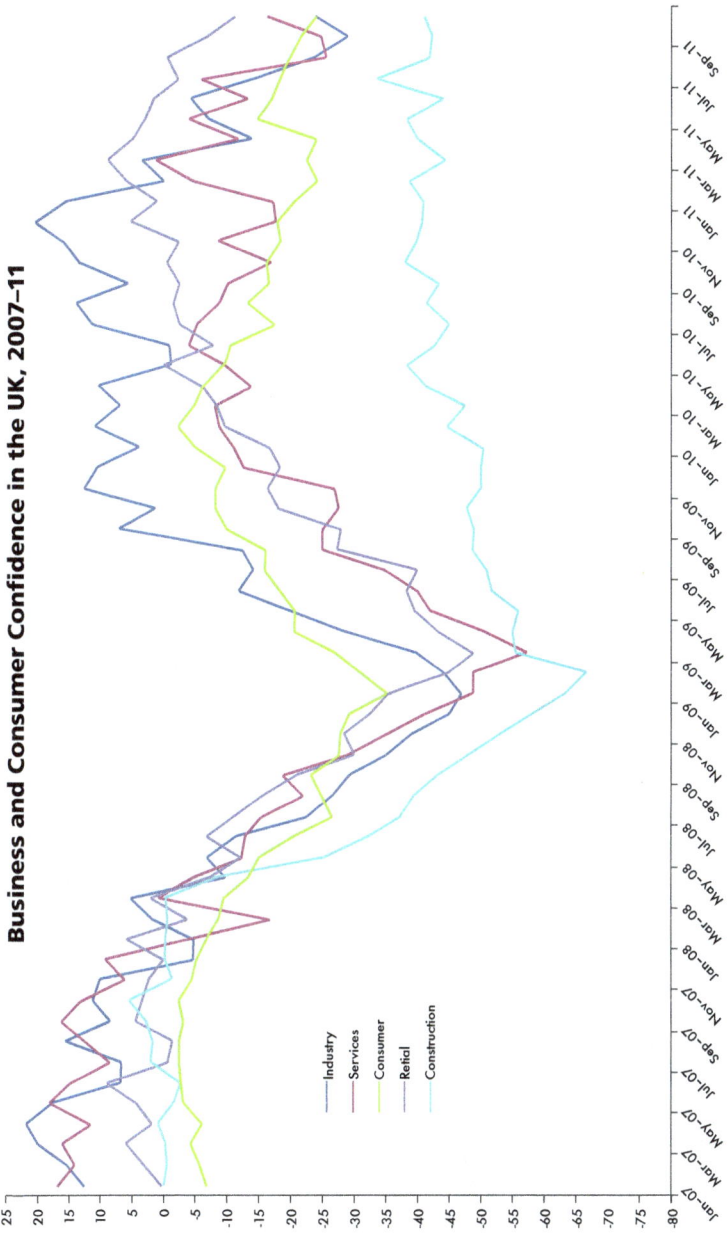

Business and Consumer Confidence in the UK, 2007–11

The October 2011 survey from the Confederation of British Industry confirms that sentiment has deteriorated sharply among UK manufacturers, in anticipation of significant falls in activity. According to the survey, manufacturing orders and output are expected to fall over the next quarter, with firms also predicting a run-down of their stock holdings. Sentiment about both the general business situation and export prospects fell for the second consecutive quarter, with large majorities of firms reporting that they were less optimistic than they had been three months earlier. The falls in sentiment were the sharpest since April 2009. The coalition had been pinning big hopes on the manufacturing sector, not least because the 25% depreciation of the currency was expected to generate domestic growth in productive capacity. This is because of the rise in the price of imported goods which is supposed to encourage import substitution. This hasn't happened because the economy is slowing so fast and firms are unwilling to invest as the consumer has stopped spending.

Worryingly, unemployment is also rising again and employment has started to fall sharply, as was to be expected. Over the last quarter alone, employment fell by a massive 178,000, while unemployment increased by 114,000. Job creation in the private sector is clearly too small to compensate for the front-loaded job cull in the public sector that the coalition ministers took such apparent delight in implementing last summer.

The number of unemployed youngsters under the age of 25 is about to hit the politically sensitive million mark. Most worryingly, there are around a quarter of a million of these youngsters that have been unemployed for at least 12 months. Total employment of those under 25 is now 570,000 below the level it was in January 2008, despite the fact that overall employment has only fallen by 390,000, so the employment of other groups has risen. The fact that the coalition cut the Future of Jobs Fund and the Educational Maintenance Allowance has contributed to the problem. Raising tuition fees has made the situation worse, hence the recent big fall in the number of applications to university. The research evidence shows that long spells of unemployment when you are young tend to create permanent scars rather than temporary blemishes. The concern is that doing nothing will result in a lost generation.

What the country needs now is a medium-term plan to deal with the deficit and a short-term plan to boost growth. I would emphasise tax cuts to firms as the way to go, focused almost entirely on job creation, especially for the young. Such a proposal would be likely to get the support of employers as well as employees. The latest Trends in Lending Survey by the Bank of England shows that lending to SMEs continues to decline, and so credit easing as suggested by my good friend MPC member Adam Posen in a recent speech, is a good idea, but it needs to be acted upon sooner rather than later. A boost in infrastructure spending with preference given to programmes that create jobs would also be sensible.

For some time now I have been advocating that National Insurance contributions on anyone under the age of 25 should be cut to zero for two years. This would stimulate the economy and help to price youngsters into jobs. It could be accompanied by a tax credit for firms making net job hires. It would also be sensible to give tax incentives for firms to invest. I would also give a big boost to the number of further and higher education places in science, engineering and technology funded with generous bursaries for students from poor families, many of whom are being discouraged from going to university by the cost. It is better to have young people in education than on the streets.

A strategy focused on growth and jobs is a realistic alternative to the coalition's austerity programme, which has delivered neither. We can do better.

CHAPTER 2

ONLY GOVERNMENT INVESTMENT
CAN END THE CRISIS

By Michael Burke

Michael Burke works as an economic consultant. He was previously senior international economist with Citibank in London.

THE BRITISH ECONOMY remains in a crisis. The crisis is accounted for by the slump in investment. Government austerity policies have prolonged and deepened that slump which began in the private sector. The private sector investment strike shows few signs of crumbling. As a result, government investment is required to break it and to lay the basis for a genuine and sustainable recovery.

Recent revisions to GDP data show that the economy has finally surpassed its previous peak level before the recession began at the beginning of 2008. But any claim that this vindicates the austerity policy is entirely false. While revising the original data upwards the official statisticians pointed out that this did not alter the character of the crisis. In the words of the Office for National Statistics (ONS),

> "Although the downturn in 2008-2009 was shallower than previously estimated and subsequent growth stronger, the

broad picture of the economy is unaltered. It remains the case that the UK experienced the deepest recession since ONS records began in 1948 and the subsequent recovery has also been the slowest."

This is an accurate summary. The depth of the recession and the weakness of the recovery are unprecedented and both are accounted for by the slump in investment. The other main components of GDP, household consumption, government consumption and net overseas trade have all seen some increase since the beginning of 2008. Only investment, or Gross Fixed Capital Formation, has failed to recover. It is now more than £50bn below its pre-recession peak.

Consequences of falling investment

This continued slump in investment has a series of negative consequences way beyond the direct negative impact on GDP. The most obvious one is in relation to pay. The creation of new well-paid jobs requires investment, in new industries, new technologies and new equipment. Instead, because of the continued investment strike, well-paid full-time jobs are not being created and there is a growth of casual, part-time, low-paid and zero hours jobs. The very weak improvement in GDP is a product of more people working longer hours for less pay. This cannot lead to prosperity.

The renewed widening of the trade gap, the snail's pace progress on government finances, the growth of menial and low-paid jobs, are all attributable to the investment strike. Without investment, and the growth in productivity that creates, growth in output must mainly come from more people working longer hours.

Yet productivity growth has not resumed since the crisis. In fact a weak and tentative recovery on this measure was thrown into reverse by the imposition of austerity policies, as shown in Figure 2.1 below. The dotted line shows the previous trend growth in productivity. The unbroken light blue line shows the previous ONS data and the dark blue line shows the most recent revision.

Figure 2.1 *Output per hour and trend*

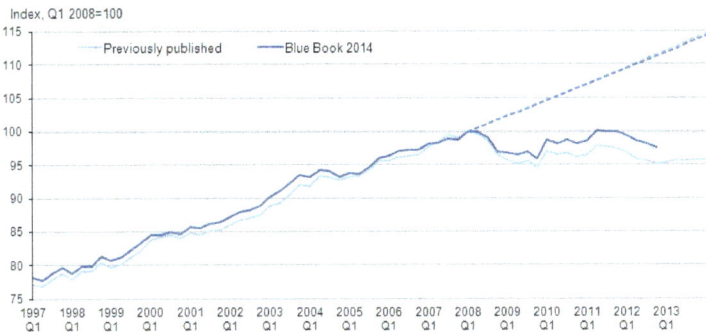

Source: ONS

This is far worse than any previous recovery. The ONS has shown that the current renewed downturn in produtivity leaves it more than 16% below the average of previous recoveries at this stage, as shown in Figure 2.2 below. The most recent data is shown in the broken black line.

Figure 2.2 *Output per hour, comparisions with previous recovery periods*

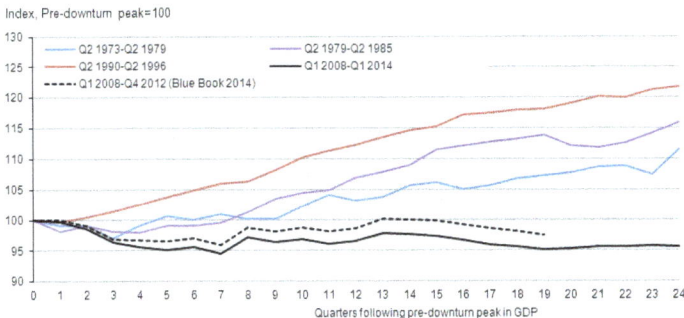

Source: ONS

21

Real wages are directly linked to the growth in productivity. Usually, the proceeds of any increase in productivity are divided between real wages and profits. Without rising productivity it is therefore extremely difficult for real wages to increase.

But the impact of the investment strike on productivity is not confined to wages, it is simply very visible there. There is too a deepening crisis of public spending. NHS waiting lists, including for cancer treatment, are reportedly at record highs. In a recent survey for the National Foundation for Education Research, Britain had the second-widest gap in attainment levels between the best and worst performing school pupils in Europe, better only than Romania. The World Economic Forum survey places Britain behind 26 other countries in the world in terms of overall quality of infrastructure. Meanwhile, the reduction in the public sector deficit is painfully slow, even though inflation has made a major contribution to raisng government revenues. The underlying deficit was £108.5bn in the 12 months to mid-2014, which is slighly higher than the preceding financial year, and only £9.5bn lower than in financial year 2011/12.

The deficit remains stubbornly high even though government has cut its own investment in key sectors of the economy. This is predictable. Lower investment produces lower returns from investment, either for business of for government. Flat productivity means increased in-work poverty and in-work benefits as well as weak tax revenues. The government's cuts in its own level of investment have deepened the economic crisis, not alleviated it. This in turn undermines any efforts to improve government finances.

In a market economy there are also great difficulties in raising social expenditure when there is no growth in productivity. In any event it is impossible to both raise wages and increase spending in education, health, transport, housing and so on if there is no increase in output per hour.

The cause of the productivity crisis is no puzzle. Just as a heavy load can be lifted much more quickly by machinery than by hand, productivity increases with the amount and sophistication of the capital machinery that is used. Cutting back on that equipment, by refusing to invest and/or letting existing machinery dilapidate will reduce output per hour. This is what has happened in Britain and many other western economies.

The argument that all that is required is increased demand is false. The final up-to-date data for the British economy will certainly show that demand, both household and government consumption have recovered since the recession. But investment has not. Increasing consumption by reducing investment is the road to impoverishment.

It is also fruitless to wait for the private sector investment, by simply providing them with subsidies to invest, which is government policy. Private firms do not exist to satisfy demand, but to accumulate profits. A number of business surveys show that firms currently remain uncertain about profits and there is growing shareholder resistance to increased capital investment.

Yet government has no such constraints. It can invest because the investment is necessary and reap returns not available to the private sector in the form of increased tax revenues and lower social security payments. State-led investment is both necessary and possible.

The role of government

There is no sign that the private sector is set to increase its level of investment spontaneously. On the contrary, a recent survey by the Engineering Employers' Federation found that 95% of respondents had made capital investment over the last two years, but only half intended to do so over the next two years.

Approximately half the total fall in investment since the recession began is attributable to private firms, while government is responsible for about 10% of the decline. The remainder is the fixed investment of private households, which is is mainly house building. While this sector is important in terms of meeting social needs and in generating employment, it is not decisive for the growth of the productive capacity of the economy, unlike machinery, transport equipment and so on. It is private firms which are responsible for the investment and productivity crisis, worsened by the government's own cuts in investment.

However, it is easy to see how this negative trend can be reversed. The biggest single customer of private firms is government. If government increases its own investment, in transport, schools, infrastructure and so on, then the private sector is encouraged to invest on its own account in order to meet new orders or contracts. This is precisely what happened earlier in this downturn. Figure 2.3 shows the relationship between government investment and business investment in the period 2008 to 2012.

Figure 2.3 *Government investment and business investment, £m*

2008 to 2012, £mn

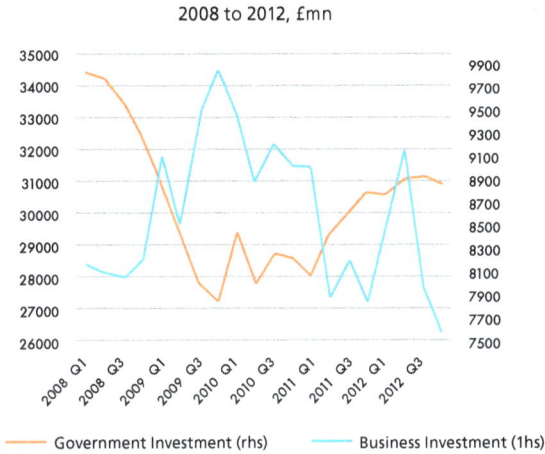

Source: ONS

The Labour government began to increase the level of investment in 2009 (bringing forward capital projects, the Building
Schools for the Future programme, and so on). About one
year later business investment started to increase. However,
on taking office the Coalition government immediately cut
its investment and again the business sector followed suit.
The evidence does not suggest private firms will increase their
investment spontaneously.

Directing increased investment

The proposal that state intervention to boost investment and
thereby resolve the economic crisis has first to confront the
ruling ideas of the last 35 years. Thatcherism argued that, by
cutting state involvement in the economy, privatising state
firms, removing restrictions on finance and imposing them on
trade unions, the consquent increase in business and entrepreneurial activity would raise growth and living standards.

The factual verdict on this ideology is absolutely clear. In the 30 years prior to the 1979 election the British economy grew by 141%. In the 30 years of privatisation, deregulation and de-unionisation, the economy grew by 108%.

This is not to argue that everything regarding the post-World War II settlement was perfect. Far from it. But the data completely belie the notion that Thatcherism or its subsequent variants were successful.

In fact, the history of the British economy is replete with examples of state intervention in order to improve the output of efficiency of the economy, stretching back to Gladstone's nationalisation of postal services in order to overcome the damaging chaos of multiple private sector providers.

Crucially, until Thatcherite deregulation every British government employed 'credit direction' over the commercial banks. This effectively set numerical targets for the private commercial banks to lend to specific sectors of the economy including transport, infrastructure, housing and so on. The banking collapse of 2007 to 2008 means that the state has now greater ownership and in many ways more regulatory levers over the banking sector than it had in the earlier period.

The banks have ample funds to lend, not least if they are instructed to redirect their current activities away from speculation into productive investment. A radical Labour government could, for example, end the Tory 'Help to Buy' scheme which has been fuelling a property price bubble and transform it into a 'Help to Build' scheme, where the same £40bn in government guarantees is applied to local authorities and others who build new homes.

There are innumerable other government schemes which in effect subsidise private sector speculation without producing any increase in investment. Scandalously, this includes a scheme to guarantee the profits of the nuclear industry which may cost up to £17.6bn. This guarantee should be ended and replaced with incentives to invest in renewable energy, which has a positive impact on the climate and creates jobs.

There are also two egregiously wasteful projects that could be cut to release funds for investment. PFI liabilities will soon exceed £300bn and drain an estimated £10bn per annum in interest costs. These provide no benefit at all in terms of service or cost-saving. Ending them would be a genuine attack on waste. Secondly, the plans to replace the Trident nuclear weapons system are set to cost £100bn on a conservative estimate. This provides no defence or economic benefit and scrapping it would allow funds for investment in productive high-tech jobs.

The Coalition government has introduced a series of regressive taxation measures which should be reversed, including the removal of the 50p higher income tax rate. But much more substantial sums could be raised by reversing the cuts in corporation tax from 28p to 20p. George Osborne argued that this measure would boost growth and investment, and so lead to higher tax returns as a result. The opposite has been the case as firms remained on an investment strike. Corporation tax revenues have fallen sharply. The return to the 28p rate would allow the government to invest the proceeds.

Some sectors of the economy are decisive for growth and prosperity, such as transport, energy, health, education and so on. The determination to hand over all or part of these to the private sector has led to higher charges, dangerously low levels of investment and poor service. In many cases, the level of public sector subsidy to these industries has not fallen, or has even increased despite privatisation.

Renationalisation is necessary in key sectors. It is unacceptable and dangerous that the private sector has allowed spare energy capacity to fall from 25% at the time of privatisation to around 4% now. In the short term, avoiding energy shortages will require even more emergency subsidies. This is intolerable and is compounded by the energy companies' refusal to invest sufficiently in renewables. To achieve the goals of keeping prices down, increasing investment and de-carbonising the economy, renationalisation is required.

This can be achieved via regulatory and other means. For example, legislation could be enacted requiring the private firms operating in Britain to invest all their profits for the next 10 years in renewables and new technologies. If this forced the share price of the energy companies close to zero, government could step in to rescue the firms by nationalising them. The argument that companies would flee could only be true of their financial capital. It cannot be true of their productive plants. The same logic applies to the rail franchises, utility companies, the NHS and Royal Mail.

This is also a hugely popular policy, with polls consistently showing two-thirds of voters supporting renationalisation of key industries, including a majority of Conservative voters.

Ed Miliband's focus on living standards is the correct one, and led to Labour rising sharply in the polls. Given that living standards for the majority continue to decline, it remains the right theme to focus on. Most people experience the stagnation in productivity and lack of investment through their own living standards. The simplest way to restore living standards for those in work is to raise the national minimum wage to the level of the living wage, and to strictly enforce it. While boosting the living standards of millions of people, the single biggest benefi-ciary would be government itself, since the majority of those in receipt of social security and other government payments are in work, not unemployed. This highlights a general truth, that the interests of a radical reforming government are aligned with those of workers and the poor.

A similarly robust policy should be adopted in pursuit of genuine equality. The most scandalous treatment of women has been a hallmark of the austerity drive, with the pay gap widening, reduced employment, greater burdens of childcare and other household burdens, reduced public services, and so on. Without any cost to government it could strictly enforce equal pay provisions for all firms. Again, government itself would be the largest single beneficiary of this. There is too a recognition that investing in universal childcare provides a wider economic benefit, which naturally has a positive fiscal impact.

Likewise this approach should inform policies in relation to the equality of black people and ethnic minorities in the economy and wider society. Black youth unemployment is at scandalous levels, and the access of all black people to public services is second-rate. The perpetual campaign against immigration is also wholly counter-productive. The strong growth produced by an investment-based recovery will both attract and require additional immigration to Britain. The alternative is to create a slum which attracts no-one.

The discriminations based on sexual orientation and on disa-bility need to be confronted. Basic human rights are being denied, causing untold misery, and the whole of society and the economy is poorer as a result.

Recent analysis from the Office for Budget Responsibility suggests that the austerity policies are only halfway to completion and that they will last until 2018/2019. Yet all across Europe we have seen electoral defeats for parties implementing austerity policies, and sometimes electoral disasters if they are parties of the Left.

None of the policies outlined above costs central government a penny. They could be supplemented with windall taxes to direct firms' uninvested profits. To be fully effective, they could be augmented by an increase in government borrowing for investment. There are innumerable ways in which investment can be generated, most of which require no government expenditure. When the crisis hit, government acted to rescue the banks. The slump is still here and government intervention to boost investment is needed.

CHAPTER 3

HOW – AND HOW NOT – TO CUT THE GOVERNMENT DEFICIT

By John Mills

A CENTRAL ELEMENT of the economic policy programme to be offered to the electorate by Labour next May, if it does well enough in the 2015 general election to form the government, is its promise to cut the government deficit to much lower proportions, and hopefully to eliminate it altogether by 2020. Admittedly, there is a caveat. It has been proposed that capital expenditure should be excluded from the calculation, although this does not stop the money to pay for it having to be borrowed and thus adding to government debt. However, whichever way the figures are calculated, there is still going to be a large deficit to eliminate. Essentially, the Labour programme – shared broadly by all the other major UK political parties – is to reduce government expenditure and to increase taxation until the deficit disappears. However, this approach begs at least two major questions. One is whether this kind of a policy will actually cut the deficit in the way in which it is hoped that it will. The second is whether, even if it did, cutting expenditure and raising taxes is the most rational and sensible way of achieving whatever target level for deficit reduction is chosen.

It may help, first, to look at the figures. According to the March 2014 Office for National Statistics EU Government Deficit and Debt Return, the total government deficit in 2013, at £92.9bn, was 5.8% of GDP. Total government debt by the end of 2013 was £1,461bn, which was 90.6% of that year's GDP.[1] Total government borrowings are not, however, rising by 5.8% per annum as a result of two offsetting factors. One is that the accumulated debt is being eroded by inflation, which ran last year at 1.7%.[2] The other is that the economy grew in 2013 by 1.7%.[3] Taking these two factors together means that as a percentage of GDP, total government debt rose in 2013 by 2.9%. This is a more manageable figure than 5.8%, but nevertheless it leaves government debt as a percentage of GDP on a rising trend which sooner or later will become unsustainable. There is, therefore, a very strong general case for bringing down the annual deficit, so that total government debt does not rise to unmanageable proportions.

Turning first to whether public sector capital expenditure should be netted off against government borrowing, of total UK government expenditure of £720bn[4] in 2013, £32bn[5] was gross capital expenditure. Thus, to eliminate the revenue deficit, on the assumption that all this capital expenditure would effectively pay for itself in future by generating enough revenue to offset the increased interest charges involved in financing it, would involve reducing expenditure in relation to income to £32bn less than £720bn. This is not, however, an assumption which can reasonably be made. This is because of the need to deduct depreciation of existing assets from gross capital formation to provide a net total which might be expected to produce an enhanced future income flow. In the UK at present the ratio between depreciation and gross capital expenditure is close to 80%.[6] Thus, only 20% of the gross figure at most should be deducted from the total deficit. Even this approach is likely to be too optimistic as the return on most public sector capital expenditure is well below the average for the economy as a whole. Taking both these factors into account, deducting any significant amount from the total deficit to allow for the benefit of some of it being used to finance capital expenditure does not look like a safe assumption. Any benefit to the public finances from this source is therefore likely to be very small.

If, effectively then, for practical purposes, the total government deficit needs to be eliminated it seems obvious that, if the government's income from taxation, fees and charges is significantly lower than total government expenditure, then the way to bring them into balance is to increase government income and to reduce its outgoings. This is the way that any prudent person would behave. Unfortunately, however, this approach involves a major fallacy of composition. What may well be true for any individual is not necessarily the case for the economy as a whole. The action taken by any individual on his or her own has a negligible impact on the totality of economic activity. This is not the case, however, for a major player such as the state, whose expenditure is easily large enough to have a major influence on its income.

There are two ways in which this linkage can be scrutinised and its effect analysed and quantified. The first is to consider the impact of increasing taxation or reducing government expenditure on total demand in the economy. Other things being equal, the inevitable result of to policy along these lines will be to reduce the totality of economic activity, causing tax receipts to fall and unemployment, with all the consequent financial implications for the government, to increase. Less income and higher expenditure will therefore evidently not automatically get rid of the government deficit. Indeed it may increase it. Of course, it might be argued that less government activity generally will stimulate the private sector to take up the slack, so that the situation will improve. This is very much the argument deployed by the current Coalition. Although employment has increased in the UK recently, however, the outcome has not by a very long chalk been the elimination of the deficit which we were promised would have happened by now. The government deficit is still running at just under £100bn per annum. A rather more rigorous view of the way the economy operates shows very clearly why this is the case, and why, with the sort of policies currently in train, neither the Coalition approach nor that of the other major political parties in the UK is likely to be effective in bringing it down.

The reason for this is that the government deficit is only one component of the borrowing and lending by four major sectors which takes place every year within the economy. The other three sectors comprise corporations – essentially all businesses operating in the UK – the household sector, which is all consumers, and the UK's transactions with everyone outside the country. All the borrowing and lending done by all these four sectors has to sum to zero, because all borrowing, as a matter of accounting logic, has to be matched by exactly equivalent lending. All these aggregates are tracked by the Office for National Statistics (ONS) and are reported every quarter in Table I in the Quarterly National Accounts published by the ONS. Set out below are annual figures going back to 2008, including those for the first quarter of 2014. It should be noted that ONS has considerable difficulty every year in getting these figures to sum to zero as a result of the need for the complex reconciliation processes required to get the outcome to balance. Especially the most recent figures are therefore bound not to be wholly accurate and in need of subsequent revision. The broad picture, however, is clear.

Table 3.1 Borrowing and lending in the UK by sector. All figures are in £m. Net lending (+) and net borrowing (-) by sector

Year	Public sector	Corpor-ations	House-holds	Foreign balance	Net totals
2008	-70,698	99,559	-40,031	11,172	2
2009	-152,053	110,173	27,779	14,100	-1
2010	-148,083	87,882	24,052	36,151	2
2011	-121,596	88,474	14,665	18,445	-2
2012	-97,962	10,378	24,179	55,445	-7,960
2013	-95,511	23,087	-4,523	67,358	-9,589
2014 Q1	-25,702	9,840	-4,200	17,363	-2,699

Source: Table I – Net Lending by Sector in ONS Statistical Bulletin – Quarterly National Accounts 2014 Q1 and previous editions of the same table Note that the figures for 2012, 2013 and 2014 do not sum fully to zero as a result of ongoing ONS reconciliation work.

This table shows all too clearly the key problems involved in reducing the deficit. To finance the foreign balance – our overall balance of payments deficit – we have to obtain finance from the rest of the world either by borrowing or selling assets, and this figure, which then appears as lending to the UK in the table above, is on a strong rising trend. It may well total £80bn in 2014. Households were quite substantial net borrowers in 2008, but pulled in their horns as the crisis developed as they then paid down debt. Now, however, they have returned to being modest scale borrowers again. The corporate sector has accumulated large cash balances over the last few years, which then have to be lent to the rest of the economy. The scale of this lending has reduced in recent years – partly apparently as a result of bank debt write-offs – and partly because of a modest increase in corporate investment, but there is still substantial net lending to the rest of the economy by this sector. This leaves government borrowing as essentially the residual figure needed to stop the economy spiralling down as a result of lack of demand.

It is now all too easy to see why attempts to reduce the deficit by cutting public expenditure or raising taxes will not work. Our balance of payments deficit – made up in 2013 by a trade deficit of £27bn,[7] transfers abroad of £27bn[8] and negative net income from abroad of £17bn[9] less a capital balancing item of £5bn[10] - is very largely made up of commitments either beyond the government's control or which it cannot for contractual or other reasons cut to any significant extent. As to other sectors, reducing net government expenditure is likely to make both households and corporations more nervous, thus reducing net borrowing by consumers and reducing investment by businesses. The inevitable result will then be that the government deficit – the balancing item - stays as high as it was before, while it may in fact get even higher. Cutting government net expenditure will not then reduce the deficit. On the contrary, all that will happen is that the borrowing and lending totals will still sum to zero but with a lower level of GDP than before as the reductions in demand from government cuts in expenditure and tax increases cause the economy to spiral downwards.

Does this mean that it is impossible for the government deficit to be reduced? No, but the only way to tackle this problem effectively is to recognise what needs to be done to change the corporate, household and foreign sector balances, to enable the government deficit to fall. The solution is not to make GDP smaller by cutting net public expenditure but to make GDP larger by adopting policies which will make the corporate, household and foreign sectors respond in ways which will bring the government deficit down. The only way to get the foreign payments lending down is for the UK to have a much smaller balance of payments deficit and the reality is that the only way to achieve this, while keeping the economy growing, is to have a much lower exchange rate. A much more competitive pound would, however, have many other advantages. It would stimulate manufacturing, exports and import substitution, thus triggering much more corporate investment and less lending to the rest of the economy. Rebalancing the economy in this way would also provide much better growth prospects, increasing consumer confidence and thus encouraging net borrowing by consumers from the rest of the economy. At the same time it would increase the amount of investment carried out by the corporate sector, thus reducing the amount of money it had available to lend to the rest of the economy. A reasonable end-state might be to have the balance of payments deficit running at £50bn, consumer borrowing at £20bn, corporate lending at £20bn and the government deficit at £50bn.

The crucial point about these numbers is that they would be both sustainable in the medium to long term and heading strongly in the right direction. If the GDP growth rate rose to, say, 4% and inflation to perhaps 3%, while the annual government deficit was reduced to, say, 3% of GDP, government debt, as a percentage of GDP, would fall by about 4% a year – approximately the difference between nominal GDP growth of 7% and a 3% deficit. Over a 10-year period, government debt as a percentage of GDP would fall from close to 100% to around 60%. Contrast this to current trends which, if policies are maintained as they are at present, are going to see total government debt rising by around 3% of GDP per annum to approaching 130% of GDP by 2025. This is a total which would be difficult enough to handle with base rate of 0.5% but increasingly unmanageable if interest rates start to rise again.

There is, therefore, a way of bringing down both the annual government deficit as a percentage of GDP and reducing total government debt. It is not to go for a policy of austerity, which will entail stagnation and misery but which will not produce the desired result. It is to expand the economy. This will get the deficit down to easily manageable proportions while incomes and living standards rise. Can there really be an argument about the best approach to adopt – especially for a Labour government?

1   EU Government Deficit and Debt Return, March 2014. ONS: London, 2014.
2   Table O in Quarterly National Accounts, 2014 Q1. ONS: London, 2014.
3   Table A1 in Quarterly National Accounts, 2014 Q1. ONS: London, 2014
4. Pubic Expenditure Statistical analysis 2013. London: HM treasury.
5   Table N in Quarterly National Accounts, 2014 Q1. ONS: London, 2014
6   Capital Consumption Report. ONS: London, May 2013
7   Table A in Balance of Payments, Q4 2013. ONS: London, March 2014
8   Ibid
9   Ibid
10 Ibid

CHAPTER 4
KICKING THE BUCKET
OF AUSTERITY

By Michael Meacher

THE PREDOMINANT economic ideology in the UK, shared tragically by all three main political parties, is that deep cuts must continue to be made in public expenditure and social benefits until the structural budget deficit is wiped out by 2019-20. By that stage, if it is ever reached, the pall of austerity will have haunted the land for more than a decade. This is at a time when wages have by 2014 already fallen by 7% in real terms, productivity is one of the lowest in the OECD, business investment is still 10% below pre-crash levels despite the FTSE-100 companies sitting on cash stockpiles of £700bn, the deficit in traded goods will hit some £115bn this year – by far the biggest ever recorded – and household debt is now tipping £2 trillions while unemployment is still over 2 million. To carry on with such a savagely deflationary policy against such a background is, to put it frankly, madness.

Of course it will be said that this ignores Osborne's 'recovery' with the fastest growth rate among the major Western economies (largely because the Eurozone under Merkel's austerity policies is doing even worse). But the so-called Osborne recovery is a fleeting chimera. It is far too dependent on a Help-to-Buy induced housing equity bubble and increased equity borrowing, as well as contingently on the massive £23bn PPI payback by the banks. It is deeply lop-sided when the only sector that has recovered its pre-2008-9 levels of output is financial services; manufacturing is still 7% below its pre-crash level and construction even lower at still 10% down. It isn't even sustainable: there are only four sources of aggregate demand – household incomes, business investment, net exports (exports minus imports), and government expenditure – and all four have been and remain strongly negative. And the 'recovery' is already showing clear signs of fading even before 90% of the population have even begun to feel it in the first place.

So why is such a counter-productive policy being pursued at all? Ostensibly the reason is to reduce the budget deficit. But it isn't even achieving that to any significant degree. Alistair Darling, deploying two stimulatory budgets in 2009-10, brought down the deficit sharply from £157bn in 2009 to £118bn in 2011, a reduction of nearly £40bn in just 2 years. Osborne's austerity budgets have slowed the reduction to a trickle, down to £108bn now – a reduction of £10bn in 3 years. So which is more effective – public investment or spending cuts? It's a no-brainer.

So if the current fetish with austerity is proving so comparatively inefficient in reducing the deficit, why is it still being pursued? The answer is that the Tory-dominated government has as its central objective, not the elimination of the structural deficit, but the shrinking of the State and in particular the squeezing of the Welfare State back to its much diminished proportions in 1948. The real aim is to switch all public services (the only exceptions being the judiciary, the armed forces and security agencies, i.e. the enforcement mechanisms of the State) to a privatised market system, and the big budget deficit, so far from being a huge constraint on government freedom of manoeuvre, has actually been a once-in-a-lifetime heaven-sent opportunity for a Tory party to complete the Thatcher counter-revolution that they could never have achieved in any other way.

What then is the alternative to continuing with this dysfunctional ideology which will almost certainly cripple Britain with desperately low levels of investment, little or no growth or rise in output per head, no increase in living standards, all accompanied by rising national and government debt, increasing unemployment and relentless relative if not actually absolute decline? The answer is very clear. There is an overwhelming need to kickstart the economy on a sustainable course of growth, and when private investment is still flat on its back and unwilling to take the lead, that role has to be played in the initial stages of the upturn by public investment. And the areas where that public investment should certainly take the lead include a major house-building programme, infrastructure development in energy and transport, and laying the foundations for a low-carbon economy.

How would all this be funded? With interest rates at an all-time low of 0.5% for nearly 6 years a £30bn investment package could be financed for just £150m a year, a sum equal to just 0.002% of annual government spending. Such a package could generate a million jobs within 2 years, increase real incomes and thus aggregate demand, boost tax receipts, and cut the deficit far faster than the current prolonged austerity. It can even be funded without any increase in public borrowing at all, either by mandating the publicly-owned banks RBS and Lloyds to prioritise lending for British industry, or by electronic printing of money (quantitative easing) targeted not on the banks (which have previously used the money for consolidating their balance sheets rather than lending to industry) but directly on industrial investment, or by a super-tax on the 1% ultra-rich.

The justification for the latter comes not only from the industrial scale of tax avoidance by the super-rich, but also from the findings of the Sunday Times Rich List which revealed (May 2014) that the wealthiest 1,000 persons in Britain today, including 104 billionaires, possess assets valued at £519bn. Whereas average wages in real terms have fallen 7% below pre-crash levels, the wealth of this tiny super-elite, which constitutes just 0.003% of the adult population, has actually doubled over this same period to a level equal to one-third of Britain's entire GDP. A rebalancing of the grotesquely unjust distribution of income, wealth and tax in contemporary Britain is urgently called for, and this would be a very apposite occasion to start that process.

But kickstarting the economy on a genuinely sustainable growth path is only the first step in the reconstruction of the British economy. There are major changes to be made in the role and functioning of the banks, in laying the foundations for a manufacturing revival, and in reconfiguring the relationship between State and markets.

There are three fundamental problems with the banks. They are too big to fail and thus involve a systemic risk to the whole financial system which could require another colossal taxpayer bailout. They serve their own interests, and recklessly at that, not the interests of industry or Britain as a whole. And they have privatised control of the money supply which has seriously reduced the flow into productive investment.

The Big 4 Banks are too big to fail when they have oligopoly control of 85% of retail accounts, with little or no real competition between them. The Vickers Commission's proposal for 'Chinese Walls' to be inserted between their highly risky investment (casino) banking arm and the regular High Street banking arm won't work because of the City of London's regulatory arbitrage. And the 'living wills' which were meant to achieve an orderly wind-down of banks in serious difficulties have been rejected by US regulators as inadequate for the purpose. What is really needed is the re-enactment of the 1933 Glass-Steagall Act (repealed, disastrously, in 1996) enforcing a complete split between investment and retail banking, plus the break-up of these over-sized mammoth banks into smaller banks specialising in infrastructure, regional development (like the German Mittelstand), science and innovation, low carbon economy, SMEs, etc.

The Big 4 Banks don't serve the British national interest because their predominant focus lies in overseas speculation, exotic derivatives, complex tax avoidance schemes, and prime location property. The proportion of UK monetary flows that they channel into productive investment has been estimated at as low as 8%, a fifth of that achieved by the Tiger Economies. What is needed is a Treasury/Bank of England guideline system, as worked well after the SWW until the market fundamentalism of the 1980s, to ensure that the banks prioritise manufacturing and exports over consumption and imports in order to lift productive investment to at least 25% within 10 years.

Most important of all, control of the money supply must be wrested back from the private banks into public hands. It was steadily privatised following the Competition and Credit Control Act of 1971 and the deregulation of finance in the 1980s. It is essential that it be restored to public control through Treasury/Bank of England directions over the broad allocation of credit to meet key national goals, and through reserve ratio requirements at the central bank to prevent the uncontrollable explosion of credit.

Second, manufacturing, on which the UK economic base depends, has been in decline for a century. There has been no surplus on the current account for 35 years, yet we cannot maintain our living standards if we're getting ever deeper into debt with the rest of the world. At the same time bringing about a major and sustainable revival of UK manufacturing requires a focused and prolonged campaign on several fronts. That must include a big expansion of skill training and apprenticeships, the extension of scientific and technical education, and post-14 vocational education; reliable sources of funding for manufacturing; the restoration of the crucial supply chains that were broken up by the privatisations and large-scale sell-offs of the 1980s Thatcher period; the necessity to incentivise the build-up of market share over short-term profiteering; the protection of key strategic sectors and companies against foreign acquisition (as every other major industrial economy deploys); and a lower exchange rate which is aligned with the price elasticities of demand.

Third, comparison of the outcomes of the 30-year managed capitalism pre-1980 era with the 30-year market fundamentalist post-1980 era points unambiguously to the need to re-fashion the relationship between State and markets. There were no financial crashes pre-1980, but 6 post-1980 leading up to the monumental crash in 2008-9. The post-1980 era led to a severely imbalanced economy: the proportion of total corporate profits represented by the financial sector tripled from 14% to 39% by 2008, producing a financial sector twice the size of Germany or France relative to the rest of the economy. In terms of stability, household debt quadrupled from 20% of GDP in 1980 to 80% in 2008, and it is now 140% and rising. In terms of competitiveness, there was certainly a big rise in labour productivity growth in the two decades post-1980, but it was not sustained. And crucially the annual growth in average incomes was 2.4% in the pre-1980 period, but only 1.7% in the post-1980 period. In other words, the economic gains of

Thatcherite deregulated capitalism did not last, but they did lead to extreme imbalance and inequality which has persisted.

What this therefore points to is the need for a new State-markets relationship which is neither centralised planning nor untrammelled markets, but rather one which learns the lessons of the highly successful post-war economies, including the Asian Tiger Economies. That implies a new role for the public sector, not only in health and education, but also in other crucial areas including energy, transport (rail), housing, pensions, and banking.

This is a programme for a generation, but nothing less will halt the still continuing relentless decline of the British economy. But the first and essential component of this programme is the repudiation of the utterly destructive and counter-productive austerity which is laying waste not only the UK but the Eurozone as well, together with the 1920s-style old-fashioned right-wing ideology of balanced budgeting on which it is based, and its replacement by a major programme of public investment, banking reconstruction, manufacturing revival, and a new entrepreneurial role for the State which together can lay the foundations for a much fairer, more equal and more prosperous society.

Michael Meacher's recently published book 'The State We Need: Keys to the Renaissance of Britain', can be obtained from him via the House of Commons.

CHAPTER 5
HOW TO MAKE 'SMART'
INNOVATION-LED GROWTH ALSO
'INCLUSIVE' GROWTH

By Mariana Mazzucato

RM Phillips Professor in the Economics of Innovation, SPRU, University of Sussex

Abstract

WHILE SOCIALISATION of risks and privatisation of rewards has been discussed as a problem in the financial sector (Haldane, 2011), the chapter argues that it has also become a problem in how innovation is funded and appropriated in the 'real' economy. Funding for innovation has become an increasingly collective endeavour, in which public funds play a critical role in the 'open innovation' model, yet returns from innovation have not run in parallel with the collective risk-taking. Understanding how to reform this dysfunctional dynamic, so that the distribution of rewards from innovation are more in line with the collective risk taking involved, will help growth to be not only 'smart' but also more 'inclusive'.

Introduction

For an 'innovation union' to emerge, 'systems' of innovation
are needed so that new knowledge and innovation can diffuse
throughout the European economy. *Systems* and eco-systems
of innovation (sectoral, regional, and national) require the
presence of dynamic links between the different actors and
institutions (firms, financial institutions, research/education,
public sector funds, intermediary institutions) as well as hori-
zontal links *within* organisations and institutions (Freeman,
1995).

What, however, has not been given enough attention in the
debate about the different actors and institutions required for
innovation-led growth, is the exact role that each actor in the
system plays along the 'bumpy' and complex *risk landscape*
(Mazzucato, 2013a). Considering these roles more explicitly,
allows us to reflect on the degree to which the division of labor
in risk taking is matched or not by a division of rewards, which
one would expect if there is a *risk-return* relationship. It also
helps us to better understand whether the eco-system is creating the right incentives. Is it the case that because some actors
are putting in a lot, other actors have been given fewer incentives to do their share?

Market failure theory discusses 'risk' in terms of the 'wedge'
between private and social returns, which may arise from the
'public' nature of goods (which limits the ability of private
actors to appropriate returns), or different types of externali-
ties (Laffont, 2008). This is the classical argument that justifies
state spending on basic research (Nelson, 1959; Arrow, 1962).
However, the mission oriented investments, which make
up about 75% of public sector investments in innovation in
many advanced economies, cannot be understood within
the market failure perspective. Missions, from putting a man

on the moon to developing the internet (which was done in DARPA, an agency of the US Department of Defense), involve both basic and applied research, and are driven not by the dynamics of the private/social 'wedge' but by direct objectives of the government (Foray et al., 2012). Indeed, the very heavy funding of the US pharmaceutical industry arises from the US government mission, through its National Institutes of Health, to 'seek fundamental knowledge about the nature and behavior of living systems and the application of that knowledge to enhance health, lengthen life, and reduce the burdens of illness and disability'. The budget of the NIH has reached $400 billion over the last decade, with $31 billion in 2012 (see Figure 5.1).

Figure 5.1 *National Institutes of Health R&D funding*

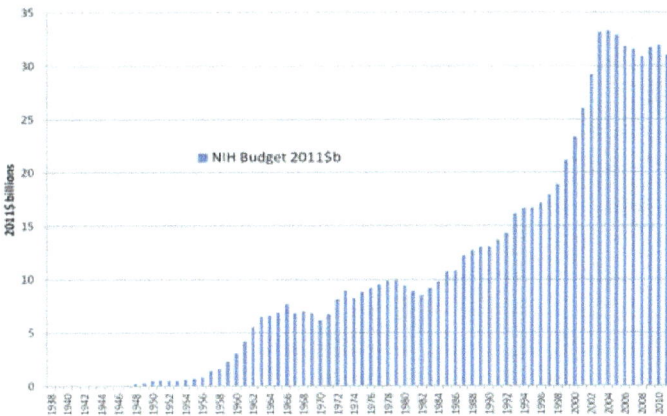

Source: *http://officeofbudget.od.nih.gov/approp_hist.html (courtesy of William Lazonick)*

At a more micro level, Block and Keller (2011a) find that between 1971 and 2006, 77 out of the most important 88 innovations (rated by *R&D Magazine's* annual awards) were found to have been fully dependent on federal support, especially, but not only, in the early phases. And all the major 'general purpose technologies', from aviation to the internet, owe their core funding to the public sector (Ruttan, 2006). Far from the often-heard criticisms of the state potentially 'crowding out' private investments, such bold 'mission-oriented' public investments (amongst a network of decentralised actors) created new opportunities, which were then captured by private initiative (Mazzucato, 2013a).

These examples are important because it is often argued that what is missing in Europe is the availability of 'private' finance willing to fund the radical technologies, as well as the specific phases in which risk is highest such as the 'death valley' stage of the innovation cycle. Yet what is not said is that private finance works well especially when it rides the wave of state investments, as it has done in the USA. Indeed, all the major technologies that make the iPhone so 'smart' are funded by public sector organisations: GPS, the internet, touch screen display, and even the latest voice activated personal assistant 'SIRI'—all owe their funding to the state (Mazzucato, 2013a). 'Geniuses' like Steve Jobs, and the presence of private VC, are fundamental, but without the state funding of (guaranteeing early demand for) both basic and applied research in the core radical technologies, it is not clear whether the VC model would work at all, and whether individuals like Jobs would have much to add their 'design' talent to.

And it is not just about research. While many associate risk-capital with either business angels or VC, in reality in many countries, including in Silicon Valley part of the USA, it has been public not private funds which have filled the high risk funding gap. In the USA, the SBIR programme, which began in 1982, provides almost $2.5 billion annually to small firms. It is administered by 11 government agencies and divided between phase 1 ($150,000) and 2 ($1 million). And as VC has become increasingly short-termist, pursuing returns in a 3-5 year period, the SBIR programme has had to step up and often funds firms that VC is too risk averse for. As can be seen in Figure 5.2, as VC has become increasingly short-termist, pursuing capital gains, and seeking early exit through an IPO, SBIR has had to step up its risk finance (Block and Keller, 2011a). Indeed, Pisano (2006) has argued that the short-termism of venture capital makes it an inappropriate model to drive innovation in science-based sectors, such as biotech, nanotech and today's clean-tech, which require much longer time horizons.

Figure 5.2 Number of Early Stage and Seed Funding Awards, SBIR and Venture Capital

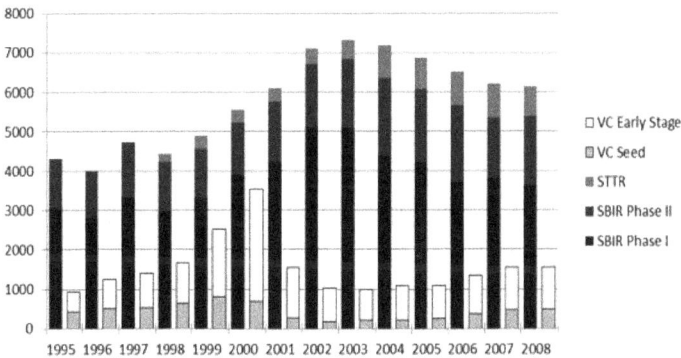

Source: Keller and Block, 2013

A dysfunctional eco-system: socialised risk, privatised rewards?

Interestingly, one of the results of this eco-system in which the state plays a leading role beyond that which has been attributed to it by either the market failure perspective or the national systems of innovation perspective, has been a fall in the investments actually made by private firms in the innovation process.

As argued by Angell (2004), the NIH has been much more 'risk-taking' than private large pharmaceutical companies, with up to 75% of the most radical new drugs (new molecular entities with 'priority' rating) coming out of public not private labs. Yet, as the NIH has been spending more and more on the knowledge base that underpins the biotech and pharmaceutical industry, the large pharma companies themselves have been spending an increasing amount on repurchasing their own stock. In 2011, along with $6.2 billion in dividends, Pfizer repurchased $9.0 billion in stock, equivalent to 90 percent of its net income and 99 percent of its R&D expenditures. Amgen, the largest dedicated biopharma company, has repurchased stock in every year since 1992, for a total of $42.2 billion through 2011, including $8.3 billion in 2011. Since 2002 the cost of Amgen's stock repurchases has surpassed the company's R&D expenditures in every year except 2004, and for the period 1992-2011 was equal to fully 115 percent of R&D outlays and 113 percent of net income (Lazonick and Tulum, 2011).

The problem is widely diffused: in the last decade, Fortune 500 companies have spent $3billion in share buybacks (Lazonick and Mazzucato, 2013). While they claim that this is due to the lack of new opportunities, the reality is that the most expensive (e.g. capital intensive) investments in new opportunities (with high market and technological risk) are being made by the public sector. In this sense, the problem is not one of 'crowding out' as is sometimes argued—because in fact the state is investing in areas that the private sector has chosen not to invest in.

And unfortunately the same problem seems to be appearing now in the emerging clean-technology sector (Mazzucato, 2013a). On the one hand in 2010, the US American Energy Innovation Council (AEIC) asked the US government to increase its spending on clean technology by three times to $16 billion annually, with an additional $1 billion given to the

Advanced Research Projects Agency for Energy (ARPA-E). On the other hand, they have together spent $237 billion on stock repurchases between 2001-2010 (Hopkins and Lazonick, 2013). What is required today for the 'green revolution to occur, is for more symbiotic public private partnerships: where in the energy sector are the equivalent of the Xerox Parcs and Bell Labs, which in the 1960s co-invested with the state in the difficult but exciting 'missions' of the future?

But the question arises whether this heavy funding has allowed big corporations to think they can earn the same or even higher profits while themselves putting in fewer resources into innovation. Indeed, pharmaceutical companies have publicly announced their rethinking of whether they need to be doing basic research at all, given that most of their knowledge comes from either small biotech or publicly funded labs (or publicly funded research in private/public universities). And they react with their feet, with companies like Pfizer closing down labs in countries where there is less public R&D (e.g. the UK where the R&D/GDP ratio is low), going to countries where there is more (US, with a 2.7% R&D/GDP and heavy NIH funding).

The widespread myth that the private sector (markets) is both more efficient than the state and the key source of innovation-led growth results in a system where the risks of investing in innovation are socialised, but the rewards are privatised. In this system, 'smart growth' does not result in 'inclusive growth': indeed, the long-term trend in modern capitalism has been one of increasing inequality between people, countries and regions, with deleterious consequences to societal welfare and environmental sustainability (Wilkinson and Pickett, 2009; Piketty, 2014). Some authors (e.g. Acemoglu, 2002) argue that the issue is that technological change is 'skill biased', so that skilled personnel are rewarded above unskilled labour, which in the extreme is excluded from the system. What the 'skill-biased technological change' fails to explain is where skills come from: in this theory, 'skill' is an exogenous factor. Other authors (Hacker and Pierson, 2010) analysed the politics of 'winners take all', in which policies (e.g. capital tax breaks) make the rich richer, while squeezing the middle and labour classes. In Lazonick and Mazzucato (2013) we go one step further and identify the mechanisms behind 'winners take all' policies, providing an alternative explanation that take into account the generation of skills and knowledge. They argue that the uncertain, cumulative and collective characteristics of the innovation process (which generates skills, knowledge and technical change) make possible a disconnection between risks and rewards. Often, actors (such as private venture capital funds and business managers) that contribute less than others (such as the state and workers) to the innovation process are able to reap a return on their investments that is higher than the risk they assumed. This leads to increasing inequality between different actors involved in the innovation process, because certain actors manage to position themselves at the point where the innovative enterprise generates financial returns (e.g. close to the final product market or to the financial market) (Lazonick and Mazzucato, 2013).

Correcting this dysfunctional system is key if we want to prevent happening in greentech the same dynamic that has characterised areas like biotech. The biotechnology industry is one where most of the VC backed companies remain productless, yet make much money for the venture capitalists when they exit via an IPO.

So if the state is so important for funding high risk investments in innovation, and given the commonly accepted relationship between risks and returns in finance, it could be argued that more thinking is required on whether and how the state should earn back a more direct return on its risky investments. That is, rather than worrying so much about the picking winners problem, more thinking is needed about how to reward the winning investments so they can cover some of the eventual losses—which are inevitable as innovation is so deeply uncertain, in the Knightian sense (Knight, 1921). Put provocatively, had the state earned back even just 1% from the investments it made in the Internet, there would be much more today to invest in greentech (Mazzucato, 2013). Or put another way, is it right that the National Science Foundation which funded the algorithm behind Google, received nothing back when Google made billions (Block and Keller, 2011b)?

Many argue that it is inappropriate to consider direct returns to the state because the state already earns back for its investments, indirectly via the taxation system. There are three arguments against this reasoning: (1) tax evasion (legal and illegal) is common and realistically will not disappear; (2) global movements of capital mean that the particular region (which could also include the EU) funding the innovation might not reap the benefits in terms of local job creation, so that the taxation question remains an open question (see the case of Apple below). And (3) investments in innovation are different from spending, on say education. The former embody a great degree of risk, similar to that experienced by private venture capital, with one in 10 investments earning a return. If the state is being asked to make such investments (which it undoubtedly has been making and increasingly so), it is necessary for it to cover its inevitable losses when those arise.

Indeed, the case of Apple computers is a case in point. Apple received its early stage funding from the US government's SBIR programme, and all the technologies which make the iPhone 'smart' are also state funded: the internet, GPS, touchscreen display and the latest voice activated SIRI personal assistant (Mazzucato, 2013). Yet Apple has employed commonly used accounting practices, which have resulted in a much lower tax bill for the US government. According to Duhigg and Kocieniewski (2012), in order to avoid taxes, Apple formed a subsidiary in Reno, Nevada, where there is no corporate income or capital gain tax. Creatively naming the company 'Braeburn Capital', Apple used it to channel a portion of its U.S. sales, instead of including them in the revenues it reported in California, where its headquarters are located. Apple reportedly saved $2.5-billion in taxes with this scheme—a very large number given the $9.2 billion state deficit California experienced in 2009. In other words, the entire state budget deficit would have been significantly reduced (by more than 25%) if Apple had fully reported its U.S. revenues in the state where a significant portion of its value (discovery, design, sales, marketing, etc.) was created and achieved (Duhigg and Kocieniewski, 2012). These facts simply reinforce that the tax system is not one that can be relied on for recouping investments, in this case by the state of California, in risky innovation. As argued by Lazonick, Mazzucato and Tulum (2013), avoiding taxes or promoting share-buybacks programmes (as announced by Apple in April 2013) are the symptoms of Apple's embracing shareholder-value ideology, which resulted in the adoption of a new financialised business model.

Reinforcing or reforming the tax system is therefore a solution for a red herring. The real problem is the financialisation of the real sector (Krippner, 2005; Dore, 2008). In this sense, financial reform proposals need to include considerations as to how to de-financialise real economy companies, in order to reward value creation activities over value extraction activities (Mazzucato and Shipman, 2014). Such reform entails creating new financial structures that support the capital development of the economy (i.e. long-term committed financial capital), and also penalising speculative practices that simply extract value and causes innovation-led growth to lead to a less equitable and highly unstable economy (Mazzucato, 2013b).

Reaping back a (direct) return

Where technological breakthroughs have occurred as a result of targeted state interventions, there is potential for the state, over time, to reap some of the financial rewards, by retaining ownership over a small proportion of the intellectual property created. This is not to say the state should ever have exclusive license or hold a large enough proportion of the value of an innovation that it deters a wider spread of its application (and this has never been the case)—the role of government is not to run commercial enterprises, but to spark innovation elsewhere. But government should explore whether it is possible to own a slither of the value it has created, which over time could generate significantly higher value and then be reinvested into growth generating investments.

For example, as discussed briefly above, three-quarters of the new molecular bio-pharmaceutical entities owe their creation to publicly funded laboratories. Yet in the past ten years, the top ten companies in this industry have made more in profits than the rest of the Fortune 500 companies combined. The industry also enjoys great tax advantages: its R&D costs are deductible, and so are many of its massive marketing expenses, some of which are counted as R&D (Angell, 2004). After taking on most of the R&D bill, the state often gives away the outputs at a rock bottom rate. For instance, Taxol, the cancer drug discovered by the National Institute of Health (NIH), is sold by Bristol-Myers Squibb for $20,000 per year's dose, 20 times (!) the manufacturing cost. Yet, the company agreed to pay the NIH only 0.5 per cent in royalties for the drug.

Similarly, where an applied technological breakthrough is directly financed by the government, it should in return be able to extract a small royalty from its application. Again, this should not be sufficient as to prohibit its dissemination throughout the economy, or to disincentivise the innovators from taking the risk in the first place. Instead it makes the policy of spending taxpayers' money to light the innovative spark more sustainable, by enabling part of the financial gains from so doing to be recycled directly back into the programme over time.

There are various possibilities for considering a direct return to the state for its investments in innovation. One is to make sure that loans and guarantees that are handed out by the state to business do not come without strings attached. Loans as well as grants could have conditions, like income contingent loans, similar to that of *student loans*. If and when a company makes profits above a certain threshold, after it has received a loan/grant from the state, it should be required to pay back a portion. This is of course not rocket science but it goes against some deep-seated assumptions. And currently, with budget deficits under so much pressure, it is no longer possible to ignore the issue.

Besides income contingent loans there is the possibility of the state retaining equity in the companies that it supports. Indeed, this does occur in some countries, such as Finland, where SITRA, one of Finland's public funding agencies, retained equity in its early stage investments in Nokia. Exactly the type of early stage investments that VC has increasingly shied away from. But state equity in private companies is feared in countries like the USA and the UK (and those countries copying the Anglo-Saxon model) for fear that the next step is...communism. And yet the most successful capitalist economies have had active states, making such risky investments, and we have been too quick to criticise them when things go wrong (e.g. Concorde) and too slow to reward them when things go right (e.g. the internet).

Other than income contingent loans, and retained equity, there is of course a more direct tool which is a state investment bank. Indeed, while many have argued the importance of a state investment bank for the needs of counter-cyclical lending (Skidelsky et al., 2011), another reason why they are important is precisely to reap back a return in order to fund future investments. In 2012 KfW, the German state investment bank, reported €2.2 billion in profits (KfW, 2013), while most private banks are in the red, with many experiencing falling profits. And indeed, if/when the state institution is run by people who not only believe in the power of the state but also have the expertise around innovation, then the result produces a high reward. A perfect example is the Brazilian state development bank BNDES, which has been actively investing in innovation in both cleantech and biotechnology, and making hefty profits from the investment. In 2010 it made 21% return on equity (ROE), most of which was reinvested by the treasury into the economy (e.g. in health and education). A percentage retained by BNDES goes to a technology fund to be reinvested in key new sectors, focussing, for example, on the death valley stage of biotechnology in which private VC is so absent.

Thus rather than worrying so much about the *picking winners* problem, more thinking is needed about how to reward the winning investments so they can both cover some of the eventual losses (which are inevitable in the innovation game) and also raise funds for future investments. Going hand in hand with this consideration is the need to rethink how public investments are accounted in the national income accounting. Investments in innovation are different than administrative expenditures: the latter does not add to balance-sheet assets;

the former does and is potentially productive investment in the sense that it creates new value (Mazzucato and Shipman, 2014). When setting limits to fiscal deficits, it is therefore necessary to distinguish public debt contracted for investment in R&D and infrastructure (value-creating investments) from public debt contracts for (public or private) consumption. In this sense, financial and accounting reforms should be regarded as an essential pre-requisite for any successful smart and inclusive growth plan. Indeed, these reforms and innovation policy must be thought through together, something that is not done in most Western countries (Mazzucato, 2013b).

Conclusion

Understanding the state as lead risk-taker, opens the question about how such risk-taking can reap back a return. While many have been quick to blame the government when it fails to 'pick winners', they have been much less quick to reward it when it succeeds. It is argued here that a framework is required both for understanding the risk-taking (beyond the risk-averseness argument in the market failure approach) and for understanding how the collective system of innovation (emphasised by the national systems of innovation approach) maps also into a system of rewards. Getting the balance right will make the objective of smart and inclusive growth less about spin, and more about concrete mechanisms.

This article is a reproduction of one by Mariana Mazzucato in Chuka Umunna's book *Owning the Future,* published by Policy Network.

References

Acemoglu, D. (2002). Technical Change, Inequality, and the Labor Market. *Journal of Economic Literature, 40*(1), 7-72.

Angell, M. (2005). *The truth about the drug companies: How they deceive us and what to do about it.* New York: Random House.

Arrow, K. (1962). Economic welfare and the allocation of resources for invention. In R. R. Nelson (Ed.), *The Rate and Direction of Inventive Activity* (pp. 609-626). Princeton, NJ: Princeton University Press.

Block, F. L., & Keller, M. R. (2011b). *State of innovation: the U.S. government's role in technology development.* Boulder, CO: Paradigm Publishers.

Block, F., & Keller, M. R. (2011a). Where do Innovations Come From? Transformations in the US Economy, 1970-2006. *Working Papers in Technology Governance and Economic Dynamics no. 35.* TUT Ragnar Nurkse School of Innovation and Governance.

Keller, M. R., & Block, F. (2013). Explaining the transformation in the US innovation system: the impact of a small government program. *Socio-Economic Review, 11*(4), 629-656.

Dore, R. (2008). Financialization of the Global Economy. *Industrial and Corporate Change, 17*(6), 1097-1112.

Duhigg, C. and Kocieniewski, D. (2012). How Apple Sidesteps Billions in Taxes. *The New York Times iEconomy Series.* April 28.

Foray, D., Mowery, D., & Nelson, R. R. (2012). Public R&D and social challenges: What lessons from mission R&D programs? *Research Policy, 41*(10), 1697-1902.

Freeman, C. (1995). The 'National System of Innovation'in historical perspective. *Cambridge Journal of Economics, 19*(1), 5-24.

Hacker, J. S, & Pierson, P. (2011). *Winner-Take-All Politics: How Washington Made the Rich Richer – and Turned Its Back on the Middle Class.* New York: Simon and Schuster.

Haldane, A. G. (2011). 'The Short Long'. Speech at the 29th *Société Universitaire Européene de Recherches Financières Colloquium: New Paradigms in Money and Finance?*, Brussels.

Hopkins, M., Lazonick, W., & Prosperity, S. (2013). Soaking Up the Sun and Blowing in the Wind: Clean Tech Needs Patient Capital. Airnet working paper.

KfW. (2013). *Annual report 2012.* Frankfurt am Main: KfW Bankengruppe.

Knight, F. H. (1921). *Risk, uncertainty and profit.* New York: Augustus M Kelley.

Krippner, G. R. (2005). The financialization of the American economy. *Socio-Economic Review, 3*(2), 173-208.

Lazonick, W., & Mazzucato, M. (2013). The risk-reward nexus in the innovation-inequality relationship: who takes the risks? Who gets the rewards? *Industrial and Corporate Change, 22*(4), 1093-1128.

Lazonick, W., Mazzucato, M, & Tulum, Ö. (2013). Apple's changing business model: What should the world's richest company do with all those profits? *Accounting Forum, 37*(4), 249-267.

Lazonick, W, & Tulum, Ö. (2011). US biopharmaceutical finance and the sustainability of the biotech business model. *Research Policy, 40*(9), 1170-1187.

Mazzucato, M. (2013a). *The Entrepreneurial State: Debunking the Public vs. Private Myth in Risk and Innovation*: Anthem Press.

Mazzucato, M. (2013b). Financing innovation: Creative destruction vs. destructive creation. *Industrial and Corporate Change, 22*(4), 851-867.

Mazzucato, M, & Shipman, A. (2014). Accounting for productive investment and value creation. *Industrial and Corporate Change* (forthcoming).

Nelson, R (1959). The Simple Economics of Basic Scientific Research. *The Journal of Political Economy*, 297-306.

Piketty, T. (2014). *Capital in the Twenty-First Century*. Cambridge, MA: Harvard University Press.

Pisano, G. P. (2006). Can Science Be a Business? Lessons from Biotech. *Harvard Business Review, October*, 114-125.

Ruttan, V. (2006). Is war necessary for economic growth? Military procurement and technology development: University of Minnesota, Department of Applied Economics.

Skidelsky, Robert, Martin, Felix, & Wigstrom, Christian Westerlind. (2011). Blueprint for a British Investment Bank. *London: Centre for Global Studies*.

Wilkinson, Richard G, & Pickett, Kate. (2009). *The spirit level: Why Greater Equality Makes Societies Stronger*. New York: Bloomsbury

CHAPTER 6

EUROPE IN CRISIS – A FAILED
MONETARY UNION

By Costas Lapavitsas

Costas Lapavitsas is economics teacher at the School of Oriental and African Studies, University of London

A historic failure

THE GLOBAL CRISIS of 2007–09 delivered a sharp blow to Europe, including Germany, which suffered a sharp recession in 2008–09 as credit became scarce and trade shrunk. The true weakness of Europe, however, became clear only after worsening public finances triggered a vast crisis of the European Economic and Monetary Union (the EMU) in 2010–12. The crisis laid bare the division of the eurozone into core and periphery, a development that is completely at odds with the rhetoric of 'convergence' and 'partnership' that had prevailed in Europe for several years. The periphery (mostly Portugal, Ireland, Greece and Spain, often referred to by the charming acronym PIGS) faced enormous difficulties in borrowing from the financial markets, and Greece, Ireland and Portugal were forced to accept bailout programmes with attendant IMF conditionality. Deep recessions followed, taking catastrophic dimensions in Greece.

During 2010–12 the forced exit of one or more countries from the EMU was a real possibility, with severe implications for the monetary union and the EU as a whole. By the end of 2012, nonetheless, it appeared that the crisis was over as conditions in the financial markets gradually stabilised; during 2013–14 peripheral countries could even attempt a partial return to the financial markets, obtaining limited amounts of funds. But the resolution of the crisis was largely an illusion. Once the periphery had been 'pacified', the severe malfunctioning of the eurozone started to become apparent among the countries of the core, especially France and Italy. The reason was that the fundamental weakness of the monetary union, namely the sustained divergence in competitiveness between Germany and most of the rest, had not at all been confronted. As a result, some of the largest countries of eurozone, including France, began to confront major problems of economic stagnation, recession and weak public finances. By late 2014 it was apparent that the EMU was a gigantic historical failure, and the EU was at perhaps the worst state in its history.

The underlying weakness of the eurozone

Contrary to what is often argued, the Eurozone is hobbled neither by the absence of a state that could bring fiscal integration, nor by the unwillingness of the European Central Bank to operate a sufficiently expansionary monetary policy. The key problem is, rather, the severe restraint imposed on salaries and wages by Germany, which implies that domestic demand is kept low. The policy of Germany has brought profound imbalance to commercial relations within the Eurozone, while also deeply upsetting the flows of loanable capital. For, in the context of the single currency – which precludes devaluation of national currencies – keeping German salaries and wages under restraint has generated a great competitive advantage, thus boosting German export performance. Since the early

2000s the country has been transformed into an exporting giant: by 2013 its current account surplus stood at $274bn compared to China's $183bn. The leap in German export performance has had nothing to do with productivity growth – which has been mediocre throughout – and is entirely due to restraining domestic remuneration. Germany is currently in the grip of what could only be described as neo-mercantilism: growth derives entirely from foreign trade. The country sucks in vast volumes of demand from across the world by keeping its workers poorly paid. [1]

German policy is the result of a profound change in the tripartite relations between the employers, workers and the state in the late 1990s. The creation of the EMU in the context of what was then German economic weakness and relatively high levels of unemployment, led to scrapping the traditional arrangement of dividing productivity gains between labour and capital. At the behest of the Social Democratic government of Gerhard Schröder, the unions accepted a policy of passing productivity gains to employers in the hope of ensuring lower levels of unemployment. This policy was in line with the dominant neoliberal logic of the operation of the labour market and has shaped German wages and employment for fifteen years. Germany has engaged in fierce wage restraint, which has naturally suppressed domestic demand, but also facilitated an export boom. Much of the growth in exports was to the eurozone, in relation to which Germany acquired an unassailable competitive advantage, given the inability of other countries to devalue. On this basis, Germany has emerged as economic and

1 See C. Lapavitsas, A. Kaltenbrunner, G. Lambrinidis, D. Lindo, J. Meadway, J. Michell, J.P. Painceira, J. Powell, E. Pires, A. Stenfors, N. Teles, and L. Vatikiotis, 2012, Crisis in the Eurozone, Verso: London and New York. See also H. Flassbeck and C. Lapavitsas, 2013, 'The Systemic Crisis of the Euro: True Causes and Effective Therapies', Rosa Luxemburg Stiftung Studien, http://www.Rosalux.de/fileadmin/rls_uploads/pdfs/Studien/Studien_The_systemic_crisis_web.pdf

political master of the Europe, the main exporter and provider of loanable capital. However, its own domestic economy is weak, not least because investment has naturally remained low in a country where domestic demand has been chronically depressed. German policy can only be characterised as 'beggar thy neighbour by beggaring your own people first'.

Conservative architecture of the eurozone

The eurozone has fostered German policy-making but it has, in turn, been shaped by the emergence of Germany as, by far, the dominant country. The monetary union is based on two rigid principles, both consistent with the dominant role of Germany.

The first is fiscal conservatism, that is, the obligation to keep fiscal deficits at very low levels, which is the responsibility of each sovereign state in the union. There is no principle of systematic fiscal transfers in the EMU, and consequently no principle of 'mutualising' the public debt of member countries. Instead there are rules regarding fiscal deficits that each sovereign state is obliged to follow, consistent with a union of sovereign states based on treaties. 'Europeanism', in other words, whatever else it might mean, certainly does not imply that there is a basis in Europe for the creation of an over-arching state, since there is no 'European people' to provide the required legitimacy. The treaties of the EU and the EMU are fully aware of this fact and reflect it in the key practice of all modern states, i.e., setting the fiscal balance.

The second is monetary conservatism, that is, the creation of a central bank that focuses entirely on price stability and eschews other targets, such as unemployment or the level of economic activity. Moreover, the European Central Bank is prevented from acquiring a fiscal role and thus introducing a shadow of an over-arching European state via the back door, as it were. In this connection, the ECB is prevented from purchasing government debt in the primary markets, a practice that is commonly found among all the major central banks and which enables state debt to be sold at low rates of interest in times of crisis, thus providing liquidity to the economy. Such a practice by the ECB would imply that one member state would take upon itself some of the costs and risks of borrowing by another, and would thus partially shoulder the fiscal burden of another. There is no basis for it within the EMU and the EU.

Both principles are consistent with German thinking and interests. They imply that Germany would not be called upon to finance other member states, either directly through fiscal transfers, or indirectly through monetary policy. They also create a rigid framework for the EMU to operate as a mechanism that ensures the stability of the euro as an international means of payment, while also acting as the domestic money of all member states. Thus, the EMU is an inherently conservative structure that prevents adjustment of imbalances through fiscal and monetary policy, and instead seeks to deal with shocks and disequilibria through the flexibility of the institutions of each country, which means primarily through the labour market. Given the wholesale change that has taken place in the German labour market since the late 1990s, the result has been the entrenchment of a competitive advantage for Germany that is unprecedented. German current account surpluses have in turn meant that Germany has emerged as the largest lender in the EU, reaping the corresponding political advantages. The roots of the Eurozone crisis as a systemic phenomenon lie in these relations, rather than in the weaknesses and failures of individual member states, undoubted though these might be.

The crisis leads to hardening of the EMU

The crisis and the policy responses by the EU have actually hardened the problematic nature of the EMU, instead of attempting to deal with its weaknesses. The policy stance of the EU – determined in large part by Berlin – has included: i) provision of liquidity support to banks by the ECB, ii) provision of emergency, 'bailout' loans to Greece, Ireland and Portugal, iii) imposition of austerity on the periphery to stabilise public finances and the national debt, iv) deregulation, privatisation and a downward push on wages, and v) embedding harsh rules in the constitution of the EU to ensure draconian discipline in public finance across the union. These changes amount to a consolidation of the existing fundamental structures of the EMU, except on an even harsher basis.

Meanwhile, the underlying source of the problem – the divergence of competitiveness due to German wage restraint – has not been confronted directly. Adjustment was initially pushed onto peripheral countries, which were forced to lower wages with tremendous social costs. But the core countries of France and Italy have not undertaken a significant downward adjustment of wages, thus continuing to develop an ever more pressing competitiveness gap with Germany. The impact on growth performance has been severe, and has been exacerbated by the imposition of fiscal austerity, following the new, harsher, fiscal rules of the EU. By 2014 both countries had been locked into zero growth conditions, with substantial unemployment and unravelling welfare provision. The political implications were equally severe, particularly in France, where the extreme Right was in the ascendant. To cap it all, Germany itself faced recession as the limits of the strategy of relying almost exclusively on exports became apparent: weak domestic demand dragged the economy down.

By 2014 the structural crisis of the eurozone had reached the core. The monetary union had become an institutional set-up creating recession, high unemployment and low growth across Europe. Furthermore, adjustment in the periphery in 2010–12 has had negative national sovereignty and democracy impacts across Europe. The shock, together with policies and new arrangements for fiscal stringency imposed across the union at the behest of Germany, has destroyed the spirit of 'united Europe' and raised social and political tensions.

Is there a radical answer?

What could be done about the EMU and thus the state of Europe? The starting point is to realise that there is no prospect of reform in a direction that would favour working people and societies as a whole. Proposals to mutualise debt or to make the ECB freely purchase sovereign debt, thus enabling EMU states to borrow more easily, run against the underlying logic of the monetary union, as analysed above. The same holds for proposals to lift austerity and to adopt expansionary fiscal policy, without first dealing with the problem of mutualising debt. Proposals to promote a well-funded investment drive across Europe to raise productivity and to strengthen peripheral economies face the problem of securing the financial mechanisms that would support the investment projects. In short, ideas of reform typically refuse to recognise that the euro is not a currency run by a federal or a unitary state corresponding to a European 'demos'. The euro is the money of an alliance of unequal sovereign states led by Germany, which has resulted in significant benefits for German exporting businesses and big banks, and that is ultimately why the EMU cannot be reformed in favour of working people.

The real issue for the people of Europe is how to exit a failed monetary union that is throttling economic activity, damaging welfare provision and poisoning politics. The realistic radical option would be to return to national currencies, thus facilitating recovery of economic independence, defence of democracy and protection of national sovereignty. Naturally, reintroducing national currencies alone could not deliver these changes, but it would be a vital step in attaining them. The return to national currencies should happen without releasing economic nationalism, or relying on market forces to determine exchange rates. It is feasible for Europe to devise a system of managed exchange rates, even including a common money for the international transactions of the EU as a whole, while member states retained their national currencies.

New monetary arrangements of this type would allow for devaluations when necessary, but without resorting to cutting wages and generating recessions. For this purpose it would be necessary to instigate permanent capital controls, to introduce public banking that could begin to reverse the failure of private banking in recent years, and to replace the ECB with an institution that could act as a fund managing the international transactions of Europe internally and externally. These changes would require democratisation of policy-making, particularly in the sphere of finance. They would also require a restructuring of the enormous volumes of private and public debt that are currently burdening Europe. None of these changes would be possible without abandoning neoliberalism as the ideological framework for policy in Europe. Core countries ought to take the lead in this transformation, and the European Left ought to be at the front. The longer the EMU persists in its current form, the stronger the risk of catastrophic collapse with unpredictable political repercussions. The onus is on the Left to offer a way out of this disaster that would be in the interests of working people across Europe.

CHAPTER 7
RESTORING PUBLIC OWNERSHIP

By Kelvin Hopkins

Kelvin Hopkins has been Member of Parliament for Luton North since 1997

Introduction

THE NEOLIBERAL economic model has failed. It has brought lower and unbalanced economic growth, high unemployment, greater inequality and dangerous economic instability across the world. Successive economic crises have resulted, with more to follow. Neoliberalism does not promote public benefit or human wellbeing: indeed, quite the opposite. As Wilkinson and Pickett's book, 'The Spirit Level', has shown, the greater income inequalities now evident are correlated with greater societal ills and human distress.

Milton Friedman, the arch proponent of the modern economic religion of neoliberalism, was once challenged on television that his economic model did not advance human wellbeing. As the challenge was repeated he became angry and blurted that it was about "freedom", by which he clearly meant a freedom for the rich to exploit and profit, not a freedom for ordinary people to live decent, secure lives.

The modern drive to an extreme form of laissez-faire capitalism has a number of shibboleths, commandments which are subsumed in almost every act of modern western government. Liberalisation, marketisation, globalisation and free trade go unchallenged in the chatter of the political classes which govern our world.

But there is one more element at the dark heart of neoliberalism – and that is privatisation. This has simply put precious publicly owned assets, publicly accountable public utilities and public services into the hands of the global corporate world, to be exploited for profit, not public benefit or human welfare. It is time to restore these assets to public ownership; to bury the concept of privatisation and dance on its grave.

Nowhere has the drive to radical capitalism been more intense than in Britain. From the late 1970s, privatisation has been forced on the people of Britain, sometimes blatantly, sometimes by stealth, and is now deeply unpopular among much of the electorate. This essay sets out the case for re-establishing public ownership in key sectors of the British economy.

The post-war social democratic consensus

Expanding the economic and social role of the state was at the heart of the socialist and social democratic transformation of Western European countries that took place after World War II. In Britain, where the boundaries of the state were or should be drawn defined the division between left and right for generations, and while the Conservatives generally resisted the expansion of public ownership, for more than three decades after 1945 they did little to roll back the advances of state provision and the role of the state in the economy. Public ownership and public service provision were seen to be here to stay and were indeed great successes from which, despite Thatcherite predations, we are still benefiting to a significant extent even today.

In those post-war years there was indeed a social democratic consensus across government and Parliament and indeed across Western Europe. The mixed economy was seen to have been firmly established by the 1960s and the left looked with much satisfaction on the achievements of the 1945-51 Atlee government, and the further advances made by Labour under Wilson in the 1960s. Coal, electricity, gas, telecommunications, water and some road haulage, railways and bus services, postal services, most of education and health, civil aviation and airports, much housing and a range of essential social services were all either nationalised or municipally owned and provided.

The Conservatives may have resisted further nationalisation but the major advances of public ownership were not reversed during their 13 years in power between 1951 and 64. Steel had been something of a political football but by and large arguments about public ownership in general were at the margins of political debate between the parties, although in the Labour Party the left continued to campaign for more of it against resistance by the Gaitskell/Crosland right. Privatisation was a word that did not really feature in political debate until the stirrings of the neoliberal counter-revolution in the late 1970s and the 1980s. Few foresaw the upheavals that were to come.

Hayek and the diminution of the state

The writings of Friedrich von Hayek, who had argued that expanding the role of the state paved "the road to serfdom", were little known and generally dismissed and derided by most who were aware of them during the early post war decades. The victory of Keynesian ideas had seemed complete and the modern world designed by John Maynard Keynes and others at Bretton Woods in 1944 seemed secure. However, Hayek's ideas were taken up by Chicago School economists, and in Britain by a small group of right wing Conservatives MPs including Nicholas Ridley, and, most significantly, Margaret Thatcher. Ridley and the so-called Selsdon Group seemed briefly to capture the Edward Heath government's agenda in its early days after the 1970 Tory victory, but Heath soon changed direction, having been made nervous by among other things the near collapse of Rolls Royce and unemployment rising to over one million for the first time since 1945.

Heath and his Chancellor Anthony Barber soon began a Keynesian reflation (the Barber boom), and even expanded public ownership of industry. Rolls Royce was national-ised to avoid bankruptcy and legislation drawn up under his government, although not enacted, was astonishingly social-ist in proposing substantial measures of intervention in the economy. Indeed, during the Blair government Tony Benn amusingly prepared a draft Bill on a policy for industry that was radically socialist. This had been taken simply and verba-tim from legislation proposed by the Heath government!

But Heath lost the 1974 general elections and Margaret Thatcher successfully challenged him for the leadership of the Tory Party. The 1970s oil crisis brought economic problems and political difficulties for the Wilson/Callaghan Labour govern-ment and despite early success in addressing the country's difficulties a series of strategic political mistakes later in that government's term saw the Thatcher Tories elected in 1979. The defeat of Labour and the election of Thatcher's first govern-ment was calamitous for the economy and for working people.

The Thatcher revolution

The immediate abandonment of exchange controls after the 1979 election, a hike in interest rates and an inevitable surge in the exchange rate brought on a savage recession. Unemployment rose to over three million and one fifth of British manufacturing industry quickly disappeared.

Thatcher's earlier promise to abandon government pay restraint policies was easily achieved simply by greatly increasing unemployment and effectively eliminating trade union bargaining power. Geoffrey Howe as Chancellor showed himself to be a true neoliberal, a hard line monetarist to the extent that even Thatcher two years on was heard to express private concern about the ravages he had inflicted on industry. Modern neoliberalism had been kick started by Howe, the true believer.

Howe's successor, Nigel Lawson subsequently presided over a period of the substantial depreciation of sterling and reducing unemployment, but the damage to industry and jobs has never been fully repaired. It was then, in the early 1980s, that the Thatcher Tories began their long march to a privatised economy. Gas, electricity, water and telecommunications were first in line. Airports, airlines, buses and more followed. Former Conservative Prime Minister Harold MacMillan, by then Lord Stockton, was moved to attack Thatcher's privatisations as "selling the family silver".

Forced sales of council houses with massive subsidies from local authority housing accounts comprised another attack on the public sector, a policy which was understandably popular with millions of council tenants who were to be beneficiaries, becoming homeowners quickly and cheaply as the better-built and most desirable houses were lost to future generations in need of decent homes. Britain had put itself in the vanguard of the neoliberal counter-revolution.

The initial returns to the Treasury on public asset sales were small and soon given away; especially in tax cuts for the rich. Those ordinary people who bought handfuls of shares generally sold them on quickly at a modest profit, and the on-going surpluses that had previously accrued to the public purse now became profits for the new wealthy and corporate private owners. In privatising major sectors of the economy the government had also abandoned an important lever of economic management: prices to consumers generally rose and investment programmes in many cases, notably water, were cut as the former public assets were sweated for profit.

The greatest of ironies was that large chunks of Britain's public utilities eventually fell into the hands of foreign publicly owned companies. EDF (Electricité de France) is 85% owned by the French state, and most recently the privatised UK rail freight operator EWS has been bought by DB, German State Railways, to become DB Schenke. As for water, a recent GMB union report found that water charges to UK consumers had risen by 50% in real terms since privatisation, whilst 95% of the world's water industries remain in public ownership.

The ultimate nonsense was the privatisation of Britain's railways by John Major's Tory government. Even Thatcher had rejected railway privatisation and it has indeed been an unmitigated financial disaster. Nationalised British Rail had "worked miracles on a pittance", to quote former rail regulator Tom Winsor. Despite and perhaps because of tight financial constraints, BR had actually achieved the highest level of productivity of any railway in Europe (Report by Catalyst). BR had also handed over our railways to the privateers "in good order", according to Tom Winsor again.

New Labour – continuing the neoliberal programme

In the 1990s, Blair's New Labour came out as converts to the economic dogma of neoliberalism. Blair and Brown had some difficulty in putting their new found faith into practice, being encumbered by two forces of resistance: much of the Labour Party and the trade union movement, both of whom had retained an attachment to social democracy and a continuing belief in the value of public ownership.

Air Traffic Control was an early battleground after the 1997 Labour victory, with "part privatisation" forced through parliament in flagrant contradiction to the Party's cry in opposition that "our air is not for sale". The Private Finance Initiative, a Tory invention, was taken up with determination by New Labour, saddling future generations of taxpayers with an enormous burden of payments to the PFI companies. New Labour refused to contemplate the restoration of public ownership, even where the logic was overwhelming, as was and is the case with the railways.

One of New Labour's most blatantly ideological acts of all was imposing a Public Private Partnership (PPP) on the London Underground, resolutely opposed by Ken Livingstone and Transport for London (TfL) but forced through by Gordon Brown's Treasury. The two companies involved, Tubelines and Metronet, both subsequently collapsed at a cost of nearly one billion pounds to tax and council tax payers and with much of the work uncompleted. New Labour also forced the pace of outsourcing at both the national and local government level, with the local authority housing sector being further diminished and weakened.

Three points have been made over and again by those on the left and in the trade unions who have consistently opposed privatisation, PFI, PPP and every form of outsourcing. Firstly, public investment is much cheaper to fund than private finance, so that paying for private investment out of the public purse in place of what could and should have been public investment was simply illogical. Secondly, public accountability is diminished and even lost as public assets and services are handed over to private companies, and thirdly, the quality of service is reduced.

New Labour's drive to secure private investment in place of public was argued on a complete fallacy: namely that it is somehow necessary to keep public investment to a minimum, even to a specific proportion of GDP. This is simply not true. Provided such investment can be funded comfortably from public expenditure, there is no magic figure above which public investment should not rise. Indeed, funding PFI, PPP and other private investments is much more expensive than the equivalent public investment would be, thus putting more financial pressure on public services and the Treasury, not less.

The argument put forward that these measures of privatisation were designed to keep public investment off the government's balance sheet was utterly false, and simply cover for the government's determination to drive to a neoliberal future, a minimal state and a world governed by markets and private corporate interests.

There is risk in private borrowing for investment, not present with public investment, and profits too are taken on top of the inevitable risk premium. With public investment, required returns to lenders are a fraction of those for private investment. In reality of course, where vital public services and utilities are involved, risk is never really transferred, and knowing this to be the case the privateers cynically exploit the public purse. They sweat the assets to the maximum, squeeze out as much profit as possible, and if it all collapses in the end they know the state will have to pick up the pieces and pay the bill, while ill-gotten private financial gains are salted away in tax havens, a scenario very close to reality in many cases.

Late in its 13 years of office, New Labour also sought to privatise Royal Mail, but political opposition proved too great. Royal Mail was eventually sold to the private sector - at a substantial loss to the public purse - by the Tory/Lib Dem coalition.

Most sinister of all have been moves to privatise the National Health Service, beginning under the Major Tories with the establishment of hospital trusts in the early 1990s. New Labour was at first committed to draw back from stealth moves to privatise the NHS by abandoning Tory plans for GP fundholding. However, having taken one step back, the Blair government later moved to invite private companies into the NHS, going beyond simple cleaning contracts and encouraging private companies to begin the process of taking on health provision directly. Diverting funding from NHS hospitals to private companies providing MRI scanning was just one example.

Local authority care for the elderly has also been forced into the private sector, with hundreds of council care homes closed. Across the board, successive governments have driven the out-sourcing of public services. Britain has indeed moved relentlessly towards the 1980s vision of Tory ideologue Nicholas Ridley MP, who argued that local authorities should simply meet once a year to hand out contracts to the private sector.

All this has been driven by ideology, by free-market capitalist dogma that claims that private markets should provide public services, not the state. It has clearly been about money, vast amounts of public money being poured into private corporate pockets. Early in the Blair government, when it became clear that New Labour was bent on pressing ahead with the Thatcher neoliberal advance, the *Financial Times*, in a candid front page article suggested that the private sector stood to profit by £30bn a year from PFI and out-sourced public services.

Public opposition to privatisation and the 2008 crisis

What is astonishing is that there has been little public appetite for privatisation and much opposition. Opinion polls suggest that the majority preference amongst the electorate is for public services to be delivered first by central government, secondly by local government, thirdly by the third/voluntary sector and lastly by the private sector. It is governments of the right and allegedly of the left who have driven this revolution, ignoring the electorate's preference, not supported by them.

A decisive setback for neoliberalism was the 2008 world financial crisis. Governments who had been determined to leave all to the market were forced to take hold of their economies again, to take radical steps to get the crisis under control with bank nationalisation, amongst other things. The last time this was proposed by a political party had been in Labour's 1983 manifesto.

But in 2008 the world drew back from the abyss into which it had been staring, the possibility of a complete collapse of the world financial system. The role of government was reasserted and the ideology of neoliberalism took a body blow. Privatisation has now become very much a dirty word and majority support for public ownership is now clear. There are a number of priorities for a renewed drive to public ownership.

A Labour programme for restoring public ownership

Much to the relief of many, both inside the Party and among Labour voters, the New Labour era was officially declared to be over by Ed Miliband, following his election as leader. We are now in a new era, with Labour more open to democratic socialist ideas.

Opposition to Tory privatisation has been strong, which is encouraging, but there has been a reluctance to criticise New Labour's clear support for the neoliberal agenda when in office. There has been no obvious mea culpa and the Party understandably does not talk too much about its recent past in government.

There is now an overwhelming case for a renewed Labour Party to end New Labour's disastrous love affair with neoliberalism and to restore the Party's historic and happier commitment to democratic socialism. There is every advantage to be gained from committing now to abandoning all forms of privatisation and to the progressive re-establishment of a stronger and more coherent public sector.

Transport

The most powerful case of all can be made in the transport sector, where so much functions only with substantial public subsidy and where it has been a fiction to pretend that it was ever suitable or appropriate for the private sector. Sir Roy McNulty, engaged by government to report on the railway industry's finances, concluded that Britain's privatised railways were up to 40% more expensive to operate than the integrated, publicly owned state railways on the Continent. Public subsidies to the railways and passenger fares have ballooned since privatisation, as the private companies have pocketed the public's cash. The vast costs of the railways can only be reduced by re-establishing a publicly owned and integrated railway industry accountable through Parliament to the voters. The bus industry should be brought back into public ownership, either municipal or national, to create an integrated and democratically accountable public transport sector.

Water

A second sector which comprises a natural monopoly – and which is publicly owned almost everywhere in the world – is water. Water should simply be renationalised to make it publicly and democratically accountable and to guarantee sufficient investment for the long-term future, with any financial surpluses accruing to the public purse.

Energy

The urgency of converting to renewable energy also demands a major public role. A necessary and sufficient programme of building insulation and establishing both micro and macro generation of renewable energy simply will not happen if left to the profit-driven private energy sector, especially where those companies are in foreign ownership. Energy prices must be accountable through Parliament and the Labour leadership has wisely taken a significant and popular step in that direction. Two thirds of Britain's energy sector is now foreign owned and British consumers are simply being exploited for profit flowing overseas. In the case of EDF consumers are effectively subsidising French consumers and taxpayers. The case for re-establishing UK public ownership in the energy industry is unarguable.

Public ownership in other sectors

While rail, water and energy should certainly be priorities for a Labour programme of public ownership, there are other areas where the public sector needs to be substantially extended. Re-establishing, boosting and giving more freedom to the local authority housing sector is one obvious case. There are desperate housing shortages for millions who cannot afford to buy into owner-occupation or pay high private sector rents. A new drive to build council housing and to expand the sector with a selective programme of municipalisation is essential.

One more priority that must be given early attention is the vast and costly tangle of PFI schemes. Those assets should be simply transferred to public ownership in exchange for government stock with low fixed-interest returns. In health, Labour should take immediate steps to stop all further privatisation and reverse that which has already taken place. The repeal of Tory legislation and new statutory powers should be taken to achieve this.

Strong arguments for expanding public ownership in other sectors can be made but a long shopping list is not necessary here. The truth is, however, that the case for a larger role for the state in the economy, with the restoration of a substantial government sector, especially in the public utilities and public services, becomes stronger by the week. There have indeed been media suggestions for renationalisation in a number of other sectors of the economy, surprisingly even including the mobile telephone industry. Where the state has significant public holdings in the economy, these should be retained, especially in banking. Other areas for possible public ownership should be examined on a case-by-case basis over time.

Conclusion

Neoliberalism took a body blow in the 2008 crisis, and the world economy has been enfeebled ever since. The seeds of another crisis are already evident and future crises can only be avoided if governments begin once again to take substantial stakes in their domestic economies and actively manage their economies on behalf of their peoples. That is what they did after 1945. That post-war economic model worked and must be recreated.

During the first decades after the Second World War the public sector was strongly established in many areas of life, proving very successful and great value for money. This chapter draws attention to the failures and vast costs of privatisation, and points towards areas where a start can be made on rebuilding public provision and the great benefits it has brought and will bring again to Britain and its people.

This is far from a comprehensive assessment of the expanded role for public ownership and public service provision that should be re-established in the future, and only some of the more obvious and urgent examples are given. Plans for expanding the public sector can and must feature in Labour's plans for a future government, and would be very popular with an electorate to whom privatisation has now for many become an anathema. Labour must break with the misguided idea that market forces can simply replace democratic accountability in the provision of vital services.

It is now time to reassess public ownership, to trumpet its successes, and for Labour to set out once again an expanded role for the public sector and a more active and interventionist economic role for government in the future. In doing so, the failings and vast costs of privatisation to the public purse, to consumers and to employees should be demonstrated.

Public ownership and public provision in the post-war era helped to transform the lives of working people and made enormous contributions to post-war economic success. For a quarter of a century living standards rose at an unprecedented rate, full employment was the norm and, whilst still less than affluent, the terrible privations of working people between the wars seemed largely to have been banished.

New generations grew up in a world where health and education were free and provided as of need. The public utilities were under public ownership, many providing substantial financial surpluses for the Treasury year on year. Taxation was strongly progressive and redistributive and millions of quality council homes were built, replacing slums which were progressively demolished. Governments accepted the substantial and active role of the state in providing services and in managing economic performance. Whilst the private sector was still substantial, there was little support for a return to radical laissez-faire capitalism and the inequalities and insecurities it entailed.

The failure and dangers of neoliberalism are clear to see and a new democratic socialist era should now be established, with restored public ownership having a central role.

CHAPTER 8

END THIS PRIVATISATION DOGMA: PUBLIC OWNERSHIP IS BETTER[1]

By Ha-Joon Chang

Ha-Joon Chang teaches economics at the University of Cambridge. His latest book is 'Economics: The User's Guide'

SINCE MARGARET THATCHER came to power in 1979 the UK has led the world in privatisation. The Conservative government sold off state-owned enterprises throughout the 1980s and the 1990s – electricity, oil, gas, rail, airline, airports, telecommunications, water, steel, coal, you name it. In the worldwide fever for selling off state assets that gripped those decades, the rest of the world looked up to Britain as the guiding example.

Privatisation was halted under Labour. However, the belief in the superiority of the private sector was such that, when it brought the rail infrastructure back under state control in 2002 following a series of rail disasters, Labour made sure it did not take the form of renationalisation – at least in legal terms. Network Rail, the owner and operator of the rail infrastructure, was set up as a private company, although on a not-for-profit basis and without shareholders.

---

1 This article was first published in the *Guardian*, 1 August 2014

When the coalition came to power in 2010, it resumed the privatisation drive with gusto. It privatised Royal Mail – the "crown jewels" that even Thatcher balked at selling. However, in recent months the tide has started to turn, albeit slowly.

Even while planning to sell off almost every remaining state-owned enterprise, from plasma supply to helicopter search and rescue, the coalition has had to make an embarrassing climb-down over its plan to privatise student loans. More importantly, in the past few months the Royal Mail sell-off has been fiercely criticised. Moya Greene, its chief executive, has questioned the viability of its universal service obligation. Abandoning this would mean that customers who live in sparsely populated – and thus less profitable – areas wouldn't get their letters delivered, or would have to pay more for them: the end of the postal service as we know it.

In the meantime, the Labour party has made the lack of competition and the suspected collusion in the privatised energy industry a key issue in its promise to "fix broken markets", and has caught voters' attention by announcing its intention to partially reverse rail privatisation. Although its fear of being branded anti-business has prevented it from proposing outright renationalisation of the railways – despite the support for such a move from most of the electorate – it has declared that if it wins the 2015 general election it will "reverse the presumption against the public sector", and let state operators bid for rail franchises.

However, if it is really to overturn the privatisation dogma, Labour should do more than reverse the presumption against the public sector: it should tell people that the public sector is often more efficient than the private sector.

Even while there are many examples of inefficient state enterprises from all over the world, including the UK, there have been many successful such businesses throughout the history of capitalism. In the early days of their industrialisation, 19th century Germany and Japan set up state-run "model factories" in order to kickstart new industries such as steel and shipbuilding, which the private sector considered too risky to invest in. For half a century after the Second World War, several European countries used state businesses to develop technologically advanced industries: France is the best-known example, with household names like Thomson (now Thales), Alcatel, Renault and Saint-Gobain. Austria, Finland and Norway also had technologically dynamic state-run enterprises.

The most dramatic example, however, is Singapore. The country is usually known for its free trade policy and welcoming attitude towards foreign investments, but it has the most heavily state-owned economy, except for some oil states. State-owned enterprises produce 22% of Singapore's national output, operating in a whole range of industries - not just the "usual suspects" of airline, telecommunications and electricity, but also semiconductors, engineering and shipping; and its housing and development board supplies 85% of the country's homes. Taiwan, another east Asian "miracle" economy, also has a very large state-run sector, accounting for 16% of national output.

Posco, the state-owned steel company in my native South Korea, was initially set up against World Bank advice but is now one of the biggest steel companies in the world. (It was privatised in 2001, but for political reasons rather than poor performance.) In Brazil, Embraer – the third largest civilian aircraft manufacturer in the world – was initially developed under state control; and the country's state-owned oil company, Petrobras, is the world leader in deep-sea drilling.

Arguably the most successful state enterprise in human history, however, is the United States military, which has almost single-handedly established the modern information economy. The development of the computer was initially funded by the US army; the country's navy financed the research that created the semiconductor; and the US Defense Advanced Research Projects Agency developed the Arpanet, the precursor of the internet.

When people realise that the history of capitalism is full of highly successful state enterprises, the rush for ever more privatisation can be halted. If the Labour party puts forward this case, it will not only gain popularity in the run-up to next year's general election – it would also be doing something of lasting benefit for Britain.

CHAPTER 9

CONSTRUCTING A
DEMOCRATIC ECONOMY

By Andrew Cumbers

Andrew Cumbers is Professor of Political Economy in the Adam Smith Business School at the University of Glasgow.

Introduction

TOO OFTEN DEMOCRACY is reduced to narrow forms of participation in electoral politics. The economy – so central to the wellbeing of all – is seldom the cause for democratic scrutiny or debate. The broader public is largely excluded from economic decision-making. In a world of globalisation, real economic power is increasingly concentrated. For the UK, the most important decisions affecting all of our lives are undertaken by a small handful of people, quite a few of these located within a few miles of each other in the centre of London. An elite of CEOs and executives dominate corporate decision-making, deciding how companies operate, what strategies they choose, what markets they operate in or products they make, how these are made and where. In the broader macro-economy, the key decisions are taken by an even smaller number: a key nexus of financial and political elites in the UK Treasury and City of London determine the setting of interest rates, levels of government investment and debt, decisions about gilt and bond markets, etc.

As I will show below, this concentration of economic decision-making power has increased dramatically over the past three decades. But it is not irreversible. Indeed, the growing social and geographical divisions within the UK urgently require us to rethink the way that we do politics and economics and the relations between them. These are key issues that I wish to explore here and suggest a resolution in making arguments for radical ways that we can democratise the economy. Breaking with the UK's existing economic model means developing forms of ownership, governance and regulation that decentre decision-making to empower all groups in society.

The convenient fiction of the property owning democracy

It is often forgotten that Thatcherism was in the first instance a response by elite business and financial interests in the UK to fears that in the 1970s the economy was moving beyond their control: a 'counter-revolution whose primary aim has always been to turn the clock back and reverse the tide of collectivism, which at one time seemed to be engulfing the country' (Rowthorn 1989, 283). Although it seems difficult to imagine now, there were fears at the time of a 'creeping tide' of socialism, not just from the growth of state involvement in the economy since 1945, but also because of an increased demand in the 1970s for greater industrial democracy and democratic control over the economy (see Cumbers 2012, chapter 2).

The Conservative response was to offer their own alternative: the property owning democracy. In the first Thatcher government, the main plank of this alternative democratic vision was the selling off of council housing with over 2.2 million homes sold off between her election victory in 1979 and the Conservatives' eventual defeat in 1997 (Jones and Murie 1999). Utility privatisation became the second key component of the property owning democracy, particularly after the 1983 election. Countering Labour's own manifesto to bring more sectors under democratic public ownership, the Conservative manifesto again made the connection between private ownership and democracy, but substituting individual share ownership and consumer preferences for collective forms of ownership:

> A company which has to satisfy its customers and compete to survive is more likely to be efficient, alert to innovation, and genuinely accountable to the public. That is why we have transferred to private ownership, in whole or in part, Cable and Wireless, Associated British Ports, British Aerospace, Britoil, British Rail Hotels, Amersham International, and the National Freight Corporation. Many of their shares have been bought by their own employees and managers, which is the truest public ownership of all. (Conservative Party 1983, np)

Driving the Conservatives' political strategy was a simplified understanding of the economy, predicated on a rather reductive understanding of the works of Friedrich Hayek, the arch-neoliberal philosopher and economist. As such, it was an idealised – or perhaps a wilfully ignorant – view of how the contemporary advanced economy works, with a belief in the sanctity of property rights, individual economic decision making and the decentralisation of (private) ownership for securing democracy and human rights over state totalitarianism.

Of course, it turned out to be a very flawed understanding of economic evolution, and in particular the tendency over time for unregulated and privatised capitalisms to turn towards oligopoly. In the three decades since privatisation there has been a massive concentration of ownership and decision-making in the British economy, away both from individual shareholding and the public realm towards corporations and multinational capital. To take one indicator, privatisation and wider deregulation of ownership controls has seen share ownership by individuals of Britain's plcs plummet massively from 53 per cent of the total in 1963 to just over ten per cent in 2012 (see Figure 9.1). Going in the other direction, foreign ownership has increased from seven per cent to 53.2 per cent.

Figure 9.1 *Ownership of share capital in UK's quoted companies 1963–2012*

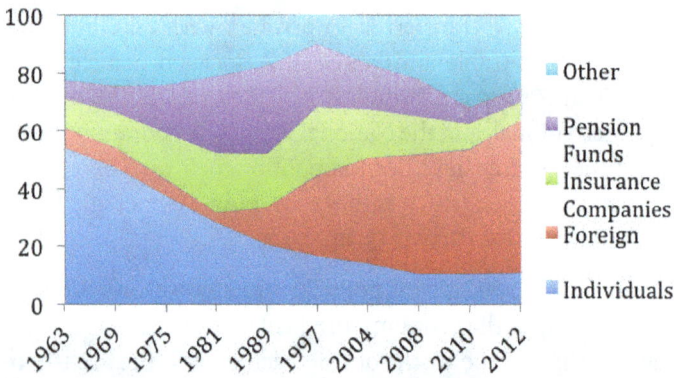

Source for Figure: ONS 2013

The result across the privatised utility sectors has been an oligopoly of foreign and corporate interests. For example, the leading four companies (Npower, EDF, Eon and SSE) account for 96 per cent of the residential electricity generation market and 71 per cent of total generating capacity (Rutledge 2012). Foreign state owned corporations account for 25 per cent of the sector but 68 per cent of nuclear power and 50 per cent of offshore wind energy projects.[1] This leads to some particularly perverse public policy outcomes – notably that Chinese, French, Norwegian and Russian governments – through their state-owned corporations – have collectively far more control over UK strategic energy interests than any British political actor.

Twenty out of 27 privatised rail franchises are operated by foreign state-owned or state-backed railways (RMT 2014), while in the privatised water industry a study in 2010 showed that ten of the twenty-three local and regional companies in England and Wales were under direct foreign ownership with a further eight owned by private equity groups including considerable foreign involvement (Hall and Lobina 2010). More broadly, the growth in privatisation and contracting out of public sector activities and the growth of massive new corporate entities such as SERCO across a range of areas from prisons, health, through to education has led to the growth of what one politician has described as "the development of quasi-monopoly private providers".

Two critical but related problems stem from the direction in which the contemporary UK economy is headed. The first is that the key strategic decisions about the economy are increasingly made by narrow vested interests rather than any sense of the common good. Private shareholder value trumps broader public interest considerations. In some other cases, we have the deeper irony of foreign state owned corporations actually using profits generated in the UK's privatised utilities to help bolster public services at home.[2] The second is that the economy

1   See Cumbers et al 2013.

2   Illustrated by the case of German state rail operator, Deutsche Bahn, where a the government's transport minister has been quoted as saying: "We're skimming profit from the entire Deutsche Bahn and ensuring that it is anchored in our budget - that way we can make sure it is invested in the rail network here in Germany" (see:

and its workings are becoming increasingly devoid of wider public scrutiny and deliberation. In a broader trend, typified by the 1997 Labour Government's decision to make the Bank of England "independent" of political interests, the economy is increasingly seen to be a technocratic sphere that should be the preserve of experts rather than the public. In what some critical observers have described as an increasingly "post-political" era (Zizek 1999), the conduct of economics and economic policy becomes completely removed from democratic control, scrutiny and participation.

The return of public ownership

Transferring more activities back into forms of public and collective ownership is clearly important in shifting the economy towards more democratic ownership and control. This is a lesson being learnt around the world as public authorities attempt to reclaim public assets and resources from the failed privatisation experiments of the 1990s. Since 2000, 86 cities around the world have taken back their water systems from privatised contractors including Atlanta, Houston, Indianapolis, Paris, Bordeaux, Toulouse and Berlin, as well as national concessions in Uruguay and Mali. In Germany, grassroots campaigns of greens, environmental and poverty NGOs, the Left Party, social democrats and even some conservatives have been involved in a remunicipalisation wave in the energy sector. Over 100 electricity distribution networks have come back under local public ownership and 44 new municipal energy companies, 'Stadtwerke', have being established in the past decade.

Driving this new public ownership wave is one common denominator. The desire by public authorities around the

---

http://www.rmt.org.uk/news/research-shows-three-quarters-of-uk-rail-now-foreign-owned/, last accessed October 13th 2014.)

world to bring core services and infrastructure back under their own control after decades of poor performance, failure to modernise utility networks, and rising prices in private hands. In the wake of the financial crisis, many cash strapped local authorities are also keen to capture future revenue streams that can fund other public services as well as much needed infrastructure renewal.

But ownership alone is not the answer. It is quite possible for entire economies to be owned by the state but still to pursue economic strategies and policies that benefit elite or vested interests without either wider public benefit or democratic participation. The experience of the Soviet bloc or China under communism after 1917 bears this out.[3] The same could be said of the recent bank nationalisations in the wake of the financial crisis which left the sector in the hands of the same financial elites that caused the crisis and failed to ask more searching questions about the relationship between finance and the wider economy.

One of the important ideological victories of the new right in the 1980s stems from Hayek's continuing dominant and pervasive narrative of the superiority of markets, private ownership and the heroic individual as defenders of democracy and liberty against the perceived evils of state centralisation, ownership and central planning. Hayek's thesis is largely discredited, given the vast inequalities of global capitalism and the increasing centralisation of power in multinational corporations and financial interests produced by free markets. The market and private ownership are no more defenders of democracy and liberty than Soviet style central planning. But his demonization of all things public and reification of all things private remains deeply rooted in the collective consciousness.

---

3   See Cumbers 2012, chapter one for a summary of these experiences

To counter Hayek from the left, we need to emphasise the way that collective and more participatory forms of economy can provide better defences of freedom and liberty than more privatised forms. In particular, there is a need for a more democratic approach to the ownership and management of basic resources, services and infrastructures which re-distributes economic decision-making power beyond its capture by financial, corporate and foreign interests. New forms of public ownership such as those described above are an important part of the equation. But they are not enough alone if they do not have the appropriate democratic and deliberative governance structures.

Creating a democratic and decentred economy

Critical to the idea of a democratic economy, decision-making power should not accumulate within particular centres or interest groups. This means institutional arrangements that foster distributed and dispersed forms of economic organisation. One important way of achieving this would be through the expansion of diverse and more localised forms of collective and public ownership (for example consumer cooperatives, community trust companies, worker owned enterprises, local state corporations) that foster greater public engagement in different economic activities. Redistributing economic power in this way does not mean an uncritical acceptance of localism and decentralisation per se but rather the implementation of the principle of subsidiarity; there will remain areas of economic life (e.g. transport, communications, energy infrastructure, macroeconomic policy, banking regulation, environmental protection) that will require higher national and even supra-national levels of economic coordination, planning and management.

Another critical aspect would be the de-centering of economic decision-making across a particular nation state, both in a functional and a geographical sense. Within any territorial form of political governance, the key decision-making functions for different economic activities can and should be dispersed. We might contrast the decentralised and federalised polity of post-1945 Germany here favourably with the growing concentration of political and economic power in the UK (despite recent devolution) around London and the south east of England. Despite the influence of globalisation, German economic organisation and institutions (most noticeably the banking sector) remain resolutely regionalised and also incorporate a diverse range of ownership models, including a strong small and medium sized private sector – the fabled 'Mittelstand' - and a health mix of cooperative and regional state forms of organisation. Decision-making power is spread therefore more broadly within the population at large and no one city or region, or elite group dominates the economic narrative.

National economic policy-making by the state should also be de-centred to encourage a plurality and diversity of institutions that are able to offer alternative and competing interpretations of economic problems. The Norwegian experience in developing their oil resources in the 1970s provides a good example of how this can be achieved. Informed by an older tradition in Norwegian society of husbanding the country's natural resources for the "whole of society" (Ryggvik 2010), the government established a national oil company, Statoil, to safeguard the national interest in the context of a sector dominated by powerful foreign multinationals.

What is less well known is that Statoil itself – while given operational freedom from government – was nevertheless encased within a strong set of institutional structures to make it open to scrutiny by Parliament and civil society. These included the creation of a separate Petroleum Directorate – significantly in Stavanger rather than Oslo - with its own powers to regulate and manage oil resources, as well as being the centre for the development of knowledge and research about all aspects of the oil industry. Additionally, what was known as the Paragraph 10 Clause was established, requiring the company to submit an annual report to Parliament. on 'significant issues relating to principles and policy' (Ryggvik 2010: 100).

The overall effect was that the company and the broader impact of oil on Norway was the subject of continuing scrutiny and debate into the 1990s. Moreover, a whole series of committees in the Storting (Norwegian Parliament) set up their own consultation exercises, including Social Affairs, Foreign Affairs and Local Government to consider all aspects of oil development, in the process drawing upon a diverse range of knowledge and expertise from all sectors of civil society, including professional association, fishing and farming interests, church groups and trade unions. Overall there was an impressive process of wide-ranging deliberation on questions of oil policy as well as collective learning so that many parliamentarians also developed extensive knowledge of oil affairs. The outcome was probably the most progressive approach to energy development ever seen which involved the following radical proposals. Norway committed itself to a 'socialized' model of oil, key elements of which were the priority that oil should create a "qualitatively better society" and crucially a 'moderate rate of oil extraction' (ibid, 34, 35) with a 90 million tonne ceiling that was not breached until the early 1990s. Additionally, emphasis was put on developing the resource in the most environmentally friendly manner as well as using revenues to boost the country's spending on international development.

The role of deliberation, tolerance and diversity in economic life

A key foundation stone of a democratic economy is the active cultivation of public deliberation, knowledge and learning about all things economic with the Norwegian oil experience above again being an exemplar. In his denunciation of state planning, Hayek made the perfectly reasonable point that central state bureaucrats were far removed from the everyday workings of the economy and thus decision-making should be made locally by those familiar with dynamic and evolving market conditions (Hayek 1948). For Hayek this meant private businessmen and entrepreneurs who should have society's resources at their disposal to respond to these circumstances. Given that advanced capitalism is becoming increasingly concentrated and centralised, one wonders what Hayek would say today. Nevertheless, the essential point about the role of local tacit knowledge in the workings of the economy is worth reflecting upon. However, this knowledge is not confined to private owners or even managers but is of course embedded within the workforce and also within consumers of products and users of private and public services. A democratic economy is one that would give voice to the diversity of these vernacular knowledges, integrating them with more technical and official discourses of economic knowledge.

Once again, the issue of ownership is important here. Spreading ownership rights and benefits throughout the population not only achieves social justice but also inculcates a greater degree of interest, participation and deliberation in economic activities. Denmark's associational economy provides an interesting example of what this might look like in practice with the growth of its internationally renowned wind power sector (see Cumbers 2012, chapter nine). As is now well recognised, this was founded upon local cooperative and community forms of ownership with state legislation in the 1970s to confine owner-ship of turbines to those living within the proximity of new constructions. This encouraged mass ownership and partici-pation with an estimated 160,000 Danish households owning shares (Shreuer and Weissmeier-Sammer 2010), representing about one sixth of the population. But it also resulted in the development of an independent turbine owners association, which developed its own knowledge and expertise independ-ent of both government and industry. Many owners and participants came from an engineering or technical back-ground so were able to bring existing specialist knowledge and experience to powerful effect in lobbying for progressive politics around energy issues. Such independent 'communities of practice' (Wenger 1998) are critical to the development of social learning agendas that can facilitate greater deliberative forms of economic democracy.

Economic deliberation and learning are best achieved in soci-eties that promote pluralism and toleration. Open dialogue and democracy require a degree of diversity and variation in economic practice. A democratic economy is therefore inevi-tably a form of mixed economy (Hodgson 1999), which allows diversity and experimentation in institutional structures. Different forms of ownership (state, community, cooperative as well as some private) all have their place in developing a more environmentally sustainable and socially equitable econ-omy for the twenty first century. Markets too have a role in consumer goods sectors, although they also have their limits as privatisation has demonstrated. A democratic approach to the economy would nevertheless ensure that markets are strictly regulated and informed by ethical practice on matters such as labour standards and rights to association.[4]

---

4   A more detailed sketching out of the contours of a democratic economy across
    sectors is given in Cumbers (2014).

Beyond institutional structures, the toleration of difference and the willingness to accept critique and dissident opinion is essential to democratic processes. Both state planning and market fundamentalism in the twentieth century had in-built authoritarian aspects in their refusal to accept alternative forms of ownership and practice. In this respect, John O'Neill has convincingly argued that markets – with their propensity towards commodification and alienation at the expense of all else – are no more a guarantor of individual freedoms or choice than Soviet style central planning committees (O'Neill 2003).

Conclusions

I have argued here that economics is too important to be left to professional economists; either in academic circles or in the City of London. Instead, we must open up the economy to greater public scrutiny, control and participation. The UK, as I have argued, is not only seeing a concentration of wealth but a concentration of ownership and decision-making power. The two threads are irrevocably entwined. Inevitably, control of economic decision-making by elites leads to strategies and pathways that favour and enrich elites and their vested interests at the expense of the common good. Thatcher's privatisation agenda in particular did not create the great property owning democracy but a private accumulation of public wealth and resources.

Developing a more socialised mixed economy along demo-cratic lines requires a radical shift in the ownership and control of resources, involving new forms of collective and public ownership of key industries and sectors. But it also needs insti-tutional structures and mechanisms that foster greater public engagement, deliberation and knowledge about the workings of the economy itself. Contrary to the views of some critics, a demand for a more democratic economy is not wishful thinking; a desire for 'castles in the air'; but can build on already existing examples from other countries in Europe and further afield. It is an increasingly urgent imperative if we are to find collective solutions to the environmental and social problems that face us in the twenty first century.

References

Conservative Party (1983) *Conservative Manifesto 1983*, London: Conservative Party.

Cumbers. A. (2012) *Reclaiming Public Ownership: Making Space for Economic Democracy*, London, Zed.

Cumbers, A. (2014) *Renewing Public Ownership: Constructing a Democratic Economy in the Twenty First Century*, London, CLASS.

Cumbers, A. Danson, M. Whittam, G. Morgan, G. and Callaghan, G. (2013) *Repossessing the Future: a Strategy for Community and Democratic Ownership of Scotland's Energy Resources*, Biggar, Jimmy Reid Foundation.

Hall, D. and E. Lobina. (2010) *Water Companies in Europe*, Greenwich: Public Services International Research Unit.

Hayek, F. (1948) *Individualism and Economic Order*, Chicago, IL: University of Chicago Press.

Hodgson, G. (1999) *Economics and Utopia*, London, Routledge.

Jones, C. and A. Murie (1999) *Reviewing the Right to Buy*, Birmingham: Birmingham University.

O'Neill, J. (2003) 'Neurath, associationalism and markets', *Economy and Society*, 32: 184-206..

ONS (2013) *Share Ownership Survey: Statistical Bulletin*, Office for National Staistics, Newport.

RMT (2014) Research Shows Three Quarters of UK Rail Now Foreign Owned, available at: http://www.rmt.org.uk/news, last accessed 20th October 2014.

Rowthorn, R. (1989) 'The Thatcher revolution', in F. Green (ed.), *The Restructuring of the UK Economy*, London: Harvester Wheatsheaf.

Rutledge, I, (2012) W*ho Owns the UK Electricity Generating Industry and Does it Matter?* Chesterfield, SERIS.

Ryggvik, H. (2010) *The Norwegian Oil Experience: A Toolbox for Managing Resources. Centre for Technology*, Oslo, Innovation and Culture.

Schreuer, A. and Weismeier-Sammer, D. (2010) *Energy cooperatives and Local Ownership in the field of Renewable Energy Technologies: A Literature Review.* Vienna, RICC Research Report.

Wenger (1998) *Communities of Practice: Learning, Meaning and Identity. Cambridge.* Cambridge University Press.

Žižek, S. (1999) *The Ticklish Subject: The Absent Centre of Political Ontology*, London: Verso.

CHAPTER 10
REFORM OF THE BANKS
AND THE WIDER FINANCE SECTOR

By Prem Sikka

Prem Sikka is Professor of Accounting at the University of Essex

Introduction

RISK-TAKING is central to wealth creation in market economies. However, market participants alone cannot be permitted
to determine the extent of risk-taking because their activities
have implications for the entire society. In a weak and permis-
sive regulatory and political environment, banks have taken
unacceptable risks and have been bailed out by taxpayers
as the government felt that the country was just "two hours
away from a financial meltdown"[1]. The government bailed
out banks by injecting £375bn through its quantitative easing
programme[2], or what many economists used to call printing
money. By March 2014, nearly seven years after the crisis hit
the headlines; the government is still committed to providing

---

1   The Independent, Alistair Darling: We were two hours from the cashpoints run-
    ning dry, 18 March 2011 (http://www.independent.co.uk/news/people/profiles/
    alistair-darling-we-were-two-hours-from-the-cashpoints-running-dry-2245350.
    html; accessed 28 February 2014).

2   http://www.bankofengland.co.uk/education/Documents/targettwopointzero/
    t2p0_qe_supplement.pdf; accessed 3 March 2014.

£948 billion of loans and guarantees to support the financial sector. This amount forms part of the officially acknowledged public debt of some £2,216.8bn which is about 132.4% of the gross domestic product.[3]

The banking crash has once again drawn attention to a rotten business culture where bending the rules to make quick profits is considered to be business acumen rather than a badge of shame. For example, following investigation by a US Senate Committee,[4] HSBC paid a fine of $1.9bn to settle allegations of money laundering for terrorists and drug kingpins.[5] Standard Chartered, another UK bank, paid a fine of over $300m (£188m) for money laundering and sanction busting.[6] Royal Bank of Scotland (RBS) and Société Générale, JP Morgan and Citigroup have been fined €1.71bn (£142bn) for participating in illegal cartels[7] in markets for financial derivatives by fixing the London interbank offered rate (LIBOR) and the Euro Interbank Offered Rate (EURIBOR). In February 2014, Morgan Stanley settled by agreeing to pay $1.25bn[8] (£765.5m). Previously, JP Morgan Chase paid $13bn (£8.1bn)[9] and

---

3   UK Office for National Statistics, (2014). Public Sector Finances, March, London: ONS (http://www.ons.gov.uk/ons/dcp171778_360531.pdf)

4   US Senate Permanent Subcommittee on Investigations, (2012). U.S. Vulnerabilities to Money Laundering, Drugs, and Terrorist Financing: HSBC Case History, Washington DC: US Senate.

5   The Guardian, HSBC pays record $1.9bn fine to settle US money-laundering accusations, 11 December 2012 (http://www.theguardian.com/business/2012/dec/11/hsbc-bank-us-money-laundering).

6   BBC News, Standard Chartered hit by $300m in Iran fines, 10 December 2012 (http://www.bbc.co.uk/news/business-20669650).

7   European Commission, Commission fines banks € 1.71 billion for participating in cartels in the interest rate derivatives industry, 4 December 2013 (http://europa.eu/rapid/press-release_IP-13-1208_en.htm?locale=en).

8   BBC News, Morgan Stanley to pay out $1.25bn to settle lawsuit, 5 February 2014 (http://www.bbc.co.uk/news/business-26043498).

9   US Department of Justice, Justice Department, Federal and State Partners Secure Record $13 Billion Global Settlement with JPMorgan for Misleading Investors About Securities Containing Toxic Mortgages, 19 November 2013 (http://www.justice.gov/opa/pr/2013/November/13-ag-1237.html).

Deutsche Bank[10] paid $1.925bn (£1.2bn) to settle the charges. A number of other banks, including Barclays Bank, Citigroup, Credit Suisse, Goldman Sachs, HSBC and RBS, have also been sued.[11] The US Securities and Exchange Commission (SEC) fined Goldman Sachs $550m (£344m) for misleading investors in a subprime mortgage product.[12] In July 2013, the US Federal Energy Regulatory Commission fined Barclays Bank $470m (£294m)[13] for the manipulation of electricity prices by its derivatives traders. The European Union is investigating the Bank of America, Merrill Lynch, Barclays, Bear Stearns (now part of JP Morgan), BNP Paribas, Citigroup, Credit Suisse, Deutsche Bank, Goldman Sachs, HSBC, JP Morgan, Morgan Stanley, UBS and RBS for possible abuses in fixing the price of Credit Default Swaps[14] (CDS).

In sharp contrast to other countries, the UK response is muted. There has been no public investigation or prosecutions for corrupt practices. In the face of government inertia, the Parliamentary Commission on Banking Standards has sought to develop some proposals for reform[15] but unlike

10 US Federal Housing Finance Agency, FHFA Announces $1.9 Billion Settlement With Deutsche Bank, 20 December 2013 (http://www.fhfa.gov/webfiles/25898/FHFADeutscheBankSettlementAgreement122013.pdf).

11 US Federal Housing Finance Agency, FHFA Sues 17 Firms to Recover Losses to Fannie Mae and Freddie Mac, 2 September 2011 (http://www.fhfa.gov/webfiles/22599/PLSLitigation_final_090211.pdf).

12 SEC press release, Goldman Sachs to Pay Record $550 Million to Settle SEC Charges Related to Subprime Mortgage CDO, 15 July 2010 (http://www.sec.gov/news/press/2010/2010-123.htm).

13 US Federal Energy Regulatory Commission, Barclays Bank PLC, Daniel Brin, Scott Connelly, Karen Levine and Ryan Smith, 16 July 2013 (http://www.ferc.gov/eventcalendar/Files/20130716170107-IN08-8-000.pdf)

14 European Commission press release, Statement on CDS (credit default swaps) investigation, 1 July 2013 (http://europa.eu/rapid/press-release_SPEECH-13-593_en.htm?locale=en).

15 For example, see UK Parliamentary Commission on Banking Standards, (2013a). An accident waiting to happen: The failure of HBOS, London: TSO; UK Parliamentary Commission on Banking Standards, (2013b). Changing banking for good (two volumes), London: TSO

the US Senate Committees, UK parliamentary committees cannot easily subpoena vital documents or cross-examine key individuals on oath.[16] In this vacuum, a series of reports by economic elites have sought to soothe public anxieties. These include Sir David Walker's report on corporate governance[17], Sir Winfried Bischoff's report on the future of the financial services industry,[18] John Kay's report on short-termism[19] and a report by the Vickers Commission[20] on banking reforms. These reports have sought to stymie reforms or appease banking elites rather than tackle the root causes of the crisis. For example, the Walker report thinks shareholders can somehow shackle a company even though they have consistently failed to do so. The UK Parliamentary Commission on Banking Standards concluded that "In the case of HBOS, neither shareholders nor ratings agencies exerted the effective pressure that might have acted as a constraint upon the flawed strategy of the bank."[21] Its general conclusion was that "shareholders failed to control risk-taking in banks, and indeed were criticising some for excessive conservatism."[22] The Kay report recognises the corrosive effect of short-termism on excessive risk-taking, which is a direct consequence of the incessant capital markets pressures to produce higher profits, but fails to tackle how these can be checked. The Vickers report calls for ring fencing

16 Technically, this is feasible but would require a vote by the entire House of Commons and is not really a practical proposition

17 Walker, D. (2009). A review of corporate governance in UK banks and other financial industry entities: Final recommendations, London: HM Treasury.

18 Bischoff, W. (2009). UK international financial services – the future, London: HM Treasury.

19 Kay, J. (2012). The Kay Review of UK Equity Markets and Long-Term Decision Making, London: Department for Business, Innovation and Skills.

20 Independent Commission on Banking (2011). Independent Commission on Banking: Report and Final Recommendation, London: HM Treasury (http://webarchive. nationalarchives.gov.uk/20131003105424/https:/hmt-sanctions.s3.amazonaws. com/ICB%20final%20report/ICB%2520Final%2520Report%5B1%5D.pdf).

21 Parliamentary Commission on Banking Standards, 2013a, page 44.

22 UK Parliamentary Commission on Banking Standards, 2013b, page 42.

investment on speculative banking from the retail side rather than a legally enforced separation, leaving plenty of scope for directors to decide where some risky operations can be located.

Some elements of the Vickers report and the deliberations of the Parliamentary Commission on Banking Standards form part of the Financial Services (Banking Reform) Act 2013, which came into force on 1st March 2014. The Act may make a marginal difference, but is unlikely to address the root causes of the crisis. Following the Act, the financial sector will still continue to be regulated by banking grandees who are too close to the financial sector. Merely replacing the Financial Services Authority (FSA) with the Prudential Regulation Authority[23] and the Financial Conduct Authority (FCA) cannot introduce any semblance of independent oversight. Taxpayers have bailed out the banks, but there is no public control or accountability of banks. The Act does little to address the addiction of the financial sector to speculation or reckless gambling, a key cause of the crisis.

Speculative banking

Banks have little interest in buying or selling houses, electricity, gas, water, copper, wheat or any other commodity, but spend vast amount speculating on the change in their prices. This drives up the price of commodities and makes people pay higher prices, but can also generate huge profits and losses. This institutionalised gambling is done through complex financial instruments known as derivatives, famously described by investment guru Warren Buffett as 'financial weapons of mass destruction'. The economic exposure of banks to derivatives, that is the hard cash needed to settle the outcome of the bets is always highly uncertain until the

---

23 The PRA is responsible for the prudential regulation and supervision of banks, building societies, credit unions, insurers and major investment firms.

contracts mature, which could be 10–15 years in the future. The danger signs have been there for years. Even the winners of the Nobel Prize in Economics who ran Long Term Capital Management[24] (LTCM) thought that they had a sure fire way of identifying winners in the speculative stakes came unstuck and in 1998 had to be bailed out. Derivatives were central to the demise of Barings Bank. In 2008, Lehman Brothers collapsed with 1.2 million derivatives contracts which had a face value of nearly $39trn (£24.4trn), though the economic exposure was considerably less. Its balance sheet boasted net derivatives assets of $22.2bn (£13.9bn), which turned out be equivalent to the bookies' receipts. As the financial horses did not reach the winning post, all of this became worthless junk and it faced claims from counter parties of $300bn (£188bn). For nearly six years before its demise, almost all of the pre-tax profits at Bear Stearns came from speculative activities. It could not continue to pick winners indefinitely and collapsed in 2008. It had shareholder funds of $11.8bn (£7.4bn), debts of $384bn (£240bn) and a derivatives portfolio with a face value of $13.4trn (£8.4trn). The derivatives gambles also brought down American International Group (AIG) – the world's largest insurer – and Washington Mutual. Then in October 2011, MF Global, the US brokerage firm which specialised in delivering trading and hedging solutions, filed for bankruptcy. It had nearly three million derivatives contracts with a notional value of over $100bn.

Despite these high profile casualties, in June 2013, the face value of the global Over-the-Counter (OTC) derivatives was about $693trn.[25] In addition, some derivatives are traded on

---

24 Lowenstein, R. (2000). When Genius Failed: The Rise and Fall of Long Term Capital Management, New York: Random House

25 Bank for International Settlements press release, OTC derivatives statistics as at end-June 2013, 7 November 2013 (http://www.bis.org/press/p131107.htm). http://www.bis.org/statistics/r_qa1312_hanx23a.pdf

recognised stock exchanges and may have a notional value of $70trn,[26] making a total of $763trn (£477trn). Others think that that the grand total could be $1,200trn[27] (£750trn). The economic exposure of this gambling is unknown and uncertain. The global GDP is around $75trn (£47trn), and it is unlikely that any government will be in a position to contain the impact of any financial meltdown.

The UK's GDP is around £1.5trn. The entire UK household wealth at the end of 2012 was estimated to be about £7.3trn.[28] Against this background, just three UK banks – Barclays, HSBC and RBS – have a derivatives portfolio, with a face value totalling nearly £100trn. Barclays leads the way with £42trn, though the actual exposure is hard to judge. Its 2013 balance sheet showed derivative assets of £334bn and derivatives liabilities of £321bn. The assets and liabilities are not necessarily hedges as the direction of exposure cannot be guaranteed. As Lehman Brothers, Bear Stearns and Northern Rock have learnt, hedges do not necessarily work in the desired way and always depend on the position of the counter parties in a highly unpredictable environment. So Barclays' exposure could be anything up to £655bn. Its 2013 balance sheet shows total assets of £1.312trn and a capital of only £63.95bn, meaning a leverage ratio of nearly 21. A decline of less than 5% in asset values will wipe out its entire capital.

26 http://www.bis.org/statistics/r_qa1312_hanx23a.pdf

27 http://www.nakedcapitalism.com/2013/03/worldwide-derivatives-market-esti-mated-as-big-as-1-2-quadrillion-as-banks-fight-efforts-to-rein-it-in.html

28 UK Office for National Statistics press release, The National Balance Sheet, 31 July 2013 (http://www.ons.gov.uk/ons/rel/cap-stock/the-national-balance-sheet/2013-estimates/index.html)

Retail banking

Retail banking has been ripping people off for years through measly returns on savings and high charges on loans, credit cards and overdrafts. The retail side invented endowment mortgage and pension mis-selling, precipice bonds, payment protection insurance and manipulation of the London Interbank Offered Rate (LIBOR). Retail banking sold subprime mortgages and played a key role in the banking crash. Northern Rock, Halifax, Alliance & Leicester, Abbey National and Bradford and Bingley were all lending money for house purchase but had to be rescued when they took on risky investments and sliced and diced mortgages into exotic and complex financial instruments.

Retail banking has not been immune from financial skulduggery. Just before its bailout Northern Rock had derivatives with a face value of £125bn. It also had opaque corporate structures using Granite Master Issuer plc, a Jersey-based special purpose vehicle, supposedly owned by a charitable trust (which did not do much charity), to book some $50bn of debt. Granite had hardly any employees, but was extensively used by Northern Rock to securitise bundles of mortgages on the money markets through bond issues. Complex corporate structures and the offshore wheezes hid risks and prevented accountability. Even now there is no requirement for retail banking operators to come clean and explain their assets, liabilities, profits, costs and employees in each country of their operation.

After the crash, banks are required to attach risk-weights to loans and to identify the capital relevant to those loans and assets. Higher capital is required for risky assets and banks must have sufficient capital to absorb losses. The choice of weights is arbitrary and unreliable, and produces uncomfortable results. For example, Lloyds Banking Group claims to have some £143bn of high quality mortgages on its books and in accordance with the current rules the bank holds some £314m of capital to cover the specific risks relevant to those loans. So Lloyds has lent some 455 times the capital earmarked to absorb the losses. It would only take a default rate of 0.2% for the entire capital of £314m to be wiped out. Despite meeting the new rules, the bank will not be in any position to withstand even a mild fall in house prices.

Reforms

1   In contrast to the Financial Services (Banking Reform) Act 2013, there should be a legally enforced separation of retail and investment banking.

2   The directors of speculative banking should be deprived of the benefit of limited liability. This way, the owners of the 'financial casinos' would be forced to bear the costs of their own failures. They would not be able to dump the losses on to the rest of society and their gambling habits would be constrained by the amounts they are prepared to lose.

3   The regulators would need to invigilate speculative banking to ensure that the gambles are matched by available capital.

4   Speculative banking should be denied access to publicly funded courts, so that taxpayers are not forced to bear the cost of disputes amongst speculators and reckless risk-takers.

5   To prevent innocent bystanders from being caught in the negative consequences of speculative activities, legislation should be enacted to ensure that no retail bank, insurance company or pension fund is able to provide any finance to investment banking without express approval from those directly affected.

6   A moderate Tobin tax should be levied at all financial tran-
    sactions. This would help to raise much needed public
    revenues for policing the sector and also discourage specu-
    lative flows.

7   Retail banks should be freed from the incessant pressures
    from stock markets for ever rising profits, a major cause of
    many banking scandals and the financial crash. Therefore,
    they should be encouraged to trade as co-operatives,
    mutuals, employee and state-owned enterprises.

8   Given the size of their loans and assets, the familiar cry
    will be that retail banks are too big to fail and we need
    to bail them out again. The proper regulatory response
    should be to break them up into smaller units so that their
    toxic effects can be contained

9   Retail banks should only be permitted to invest in securi-
    ties specified by the regulators. These would primarily be
    low to medium risk securities.

10 Retail banks should not be permitted to slice and dice or
    repackage loans and mortgages into complex financial
    instruments whose risks are poorly understood.

11 For far too long, the UK banking regulation has suffered
    from revolving doors whereby financial insiders become
    regulators and vice-versa. They have been too close to the
    values, vocabularies and agendas of the industry and have
    failed to listen to the interests of other stakeholders. This
    vicious circle needs to be broken. The main priority of any
    regulator should be to protect the financial system and the
    individual consumer and this cannot be done unless there
    is some ideological distance between the industry and the
    regulator. The regulator needs to be advised by a Board
    of Stakeholders, representing a plurality of interests. This
    Board shall not be dominated by the finance industry. In

fact, only a minority shall come from the industry thus ensuring that other voices are heard. Its meetings would be held in the open and its minutes and working papers would be publicly available.

12   Banks are global and the current financial crisis has shown the difficulties for a single state to contain the toxic effects of the crisis. As multinational corporations banks are also likely to arbitrage on regulation and thus may escape the full extent of regulation. There is need for effective international co-ordination. The UK should join the EU wide supervision of financial institutions.

13   A poorly regulated shadow banking system has sprung up. It is estimated to be worth some $71trn[29] (£44.4trn) and mainly consists of hedge funds, private equity, money market funds, trust companies, pawn brokers and structured investment vehicles. The system is located in rich economies. The US accounts for $23trn, the euro zone $22trn and the UK $9trn (£5.63trn) of the amounts associated with shadow banking system. Poor regulation was a deliberate political choice even though the system used short term wealth management projects to shift finance and devised transactions that keep vast swathes of assets and liabilities off banking balance sheets. Such sectors need to be subjected to the full rigours of the formal banking regulations.

14   The global financial architecture needs to be reformed. The current G20 forum is concerned with international financial stability and examines issues that go beyond the jurisdiction of one state. However, it is very narrowly conceived and has done little to address the trade and investment imbalances, or regulate shadow banking, a major reason for the flight

---

29 Financial Stability Board, (2013). Global Shadow Banking Monitoring Report 2013, Basel: Bank for International Settlements.

of capital and rampant credit which is increasingly disconnected from the real economy. Many states are excluded. For example, Norway is the seventh largest contributor to international development programmes organised by United Nations. It is not a member of the EU and does not have a direct or indirect representation in the G20. Similarly, around another 170 nations are excluded from the forum and have little say in the design and operations of the global financial architecture. Instead of an elite group plotting policies to advance its own self-interest, a Global Economic Council under the auspices of United Nations should be established to ensure that the world of finance connects with the lived experiences of the people and that the financial sector cannot find new shadowy nooks and crannies to obfuscate its operations. Unlike the current arrangements, the revised system should operate under a clear formal charter and the minutes of its meetings should be publicly available.

15 Other international financial institutions, such as the International Monetary Fund and the World Bank should also be reformed to make them democratic and accountable.

16 All financial products should be tested by banks and the regulator before being launched. Their capacity to cause destruction should be examined. The results of all tests should be publicly available.

17 In pursuit of higher returns for shareholders, banks have taken on excessive leverage. The key reason for this is that the interest paid on corporate debt attracts tax relief, currently at the rate of 21%. The tax policy should be neutral. The payment of dividends does not attract tax relief for corporations. The same should also apply to the payment of interest on debt too. Thus directors' decision on whether to finance investment with debt from borrowing

would purely be governed by commercial considerations rather than the hidden subsidy from taxpayers.

18   The regulators need to force banks to reduce their leverage and increase liquidity. Rather than requiring banks to restrain executive pay and dividends to build their capital base, the latest Basel accord (Basel III) requires them to have a leverage ratio of only 3%,[30] roughly equivalent to the financial position of RBS which prompted a state-sponsored rescue. This appeases the banking lobby and does nothing to address risk-taking. The banks' preference for high leverage means that small downturns can wipe out their capital. The key goal should be stability and that cannot be achieved with high leverage ratios. We would argue that banks should have at least 15% equity.

19   The executive remuneration contracts at all banks should be publically available. Employees, borrowers and lenders at all banks should be empowered to vote on executive remuneration. Their vote shall be binding.

20   Bank executives should get a basic salary. Any additional bonuses or incentives, if any, should require a binding vote from employees, borrowers and savers. The incentives should be linked to matters which emphasise long-term factors, such as freedom from scandals, service to community, maintaining branch networks, consumer satisfaction, loans to small businesses, universal and fair access to finance, innovation and investment. The bonuses, if awarded, would be payable after five years and the agreements shall contain clauses for clawbacks. This would enable a focus on the medium/long term.

---

30   Bloomberg, Basel Regulators Ease Leverage-Ratio Rule for Banks, 13 January 2014 (http://www.bloomberg.com/news/2014-01-12/banks-get-scaled-back-rule-on-debt-limit-from-basel-regulators.html).

21 Banks should rebuild their capital base by controlling executive remuneration and dividends.

22 Banks should be part of local communities. They should not be permitted to up sticks and leave local communities in the lurch. Maintaining a socially desirable network of branches should be a necessary quid pro quo for a deposit-taking licence and the state's deposit protection guarantee. Each branch closure must be sanctioned by the regulator and banks must be required to demonstrate that after closure the local community's access to banking services will not suffer.

23 Banks must not be permitted to obfuscate their accountability by hiding behind offshore operations or spurious special purpose vehicles. Each direct or indirect offshore excursion must be specifically approved by the regulator. Complete details must be provided and a report showing their assets, liabilities, profits, losses, capital, taxes and employees in each jurisdiction of their operations must be published.

24 The commercial credit rating agencies have failed to highlight the risks of securities. They promote corporate securities and inevitably have a fee dependency on clients. There are too many conflicts of interests. These should be tackled by establishing an EU wide credit rating agency. This may delegate some tasks, under strict conditions, to commercial operators. All credit rating agencies should disclose the models used to assign credit ratings and provide details of their methodologies. The credit rating assigned to any financial product should be regularly revisited. Details of all contracts and relationships between banks and credit rating agencies should be publicly available.

25 Banks have been significant players in the tax avoidance industry and have also avoided taxes on their own profits. This should be checked by making their tax returns publicly available. They should be required to publish complete details of any tax avoidance, for themselves or their clients, facilitated through their operations.

26 The private sector auditors of banks have failed. Despite queues outside Northern Rock and demise of many US banks, all major banks received unqualified audit opinions from PricewaterhouseCoopers, Deloitte & Touche, KPMG and Ernst & Young. Private sector auditors have a history of silence and are immersed in too many conflicts of interests, as evidenced by their silence at Barings, Bank of Credit and Commerce International (BCCI) and other debacles. Accounting firms have shown no interest in serving the public or the state. The audits of all banks should be carried out on a real-time basis directly by the regulator, or an agency specifically created for that purpose. This would enhance the regulator's knowledge base and capacity for timely interventions. In the era of instant movement of money ex-post audits are of little use.

27 Currently, accounting standards for banks are set by the International Accounting Standards Board (IASB), a private limited company based in London and funded by the Big Four accounting firms, who audit banks, and major corporations. The rules have enabled banks to publish opaque annual accounts. Vast amounts of assets and liabilities have not been shown on their balance sheets. Many toxic assets have continued to be shown in bank balance sheets as good assets. Despite higher risks and falling credit worthiness they have been able to inflate their profits with spurious adjustments, such as debt valuation adjustments. As a result, markets, investors, savers and regulators have been misled. Accountings standards for banks must be

set by a body independent of the financial sector and the accounting industry. The rules should be set by the regulator and approved by the House of Commons Treasury Committee.

28 Banks have been very adept at lobbying to resist legislation. Much of their lobbying power remains hidden from public scrutiny. To guard against softer regulation, all banks should be required to publish the names of the lobbyists used, public office, if any held by the lobbyists during the previous five years, the public officials lobbied, details of lobbying and amounts spent on lobbying.

29 The House of Commons Treasury Committee should hold an annual hearing into banking regulation to ensure that regulators are diligently and effectively performing their tasks. In common with other parliamentary committees, it should have the powers to subpoena documents relevant to its investigations and cross-examine witnesses under oath.

The above reforms are not a silver bullet, but will help to reduce speculative activity and quarantine the negative effects of reckless gambling. They provide hands-on regulation and will enhance bank and regulator accountability.

CHAPTER 11
ENHANCING THE ROLE
OF THE UNIONS

By Len McCluskey

Len McCluskey is General Secretary of the trade union Unite

THE BIGGEST ISSUE confronting our unions and their members over the past 30 years has not been the sharp decline of trade union membership and density, but the even sharper decline of a key economic function performed by trade unions – the precipitous collapse of the coverage of collective bargaining.

When the last Conservative government of Margaret Thatcher came to office in 1979 82% of workers in the UK had their main terms and conditions determined by a union-negotiated collective agreement. Now, the latest figures show that this coverage is down to 23%. The result is that the share of national income going to salaries and wages has fallen from 65% in 1980 to 53% in 2012.

Looked at another way, the top 1% of UK earners currently pay 30% of income tax. But when Thatcher came in, this same 1% only paid 11% of the total tax take – the reason being that incomes were more dispersed. Now they're concentrated at the top.

This decline in the share of national income going to working people is directly correlated with the precipitous decline in collective bargaining coverage. There can be no other reasonable explanation. So why has collective bargaining collapsed?

The collapse in trade union membership from 55% of the workforce in 1979 to 23.2% in 2012 is only part of the answer.

The answer lies partly with the anti-union laws introduced in the 1980s and 1990s, and partly because the state has withdrawn support for collective bargaining as part of the free market ideology, which seeks the deregulation of all markets, including the labour market.

It's ironic – to say the least – that deregulation of the labour market requires the tightest regulation of one of the key players in that market: the trade union movement.

We can't say that we weren't warned about the Right's distaste for collective bargaining. The neoliberal counter-revolution has had a long gestation period.

Mrs Thatcher's favourite guru, Professor Hayek, wrote in 1960 that the elimination of collective bargaining had to be a top priority: "It would be necessary ... to rescind all legal provisions which make contracts concluded with the representatives of the majority of workers of a plant or industry binding on all employees and to deprive all organised groups of any right of concluding contracts binding on men who have not voluntarily delegated this authority to them".

It is right that the enhancement of the National Minimum Wage into a Living Wage would lift many workers in the poorly-organised and almost informal sections of the labour market out of poverty. However, it is collective bargaining that would have a real redistributive effect, as the lack of it has shown by the concentration of income among the already well off.

Individual rights at work

Strangely then, when the Cameron government assumed office in 2010, the Prime Minister was reported as saying that the government had no plans to legislate further on trade unions. This turned out to be an untruth to say the least. What the government did do – with Vince Cable religiously following the path set for him by the man behind Wonga payday loans Adrian Beecroft – was to launch an assault on individual rights at work.

These rights, many of which date from the late 1960s and early 1970s, were often introduced as a way of heading off trade union militancy.

Vince Cable's big launch was in November 2011 when he announced a 15-point reform plan, including:

- Fees for anyone wishing to take a claim to an Employment Tribunal (£1,200 for unfair dismissal);
- Increasing the qualification period for unfair dismissal from one to two years;
- Reducing the statutory period for collective redundancy consultations from 90 days to 45 days;
- Raising the possibility of "compensated no fault dismissal" for firms with fewer than 10 employees – which dropped;
- Speculating about introducing "protected conversations", which would have allowed employers to discuss issues like retirement or poor performance with staff – without this being used in any subsequent Tribunal claim;

- Requiring all cases bound for the ET to be diverted to the Advisory, Conciliation and Arbitration Service (ACAS), in order to be offered pre-claim conciliation before being allowed to proceed to the Tribunal;

- Arguing for the simplification of compromise agreements, which now have been renamed "settlement agreements" – the terms of reference of which have been changed to allow "compensated no fault dismissal" by another means.

Labour, led by Ian Murray MP, opposed most of the Beecroft proposals as they passed through Parliament, mainly as the Enterprise & Regulatory Reform Act, so we may expect some progress on individual rights at work from the incoming Labour government.

Rights for shares

The government has not had everything its own way with employment rights reform. The first reverse it suffered was with a policy clearly identified with Chancellor George Osborne.

In 2012, Osborne outlined plans not only to further erode employment rights but also to change the status of "employee" to some other sort of worker who would have a stake in the equity of the enterprise. This is now part of the Growth & Infrastructure Act 2013.

Employers are now able to make new job offers conditional on – and offer existing staff – this new arrangement. Employees will be given at least £2,000 in shares in the business, exempt from capital gains tax when they sell.

In return, the employees will give up their rights on:

- Unfair dismissal;

- Statutory redundancy;
- The right to request flexible working and time off for training.

They will also be required to provide 16 weeks' notice of a firm date of return from maternity leave, instead of the current eight.

The unions and most major employers have had nothing to do with this – a flagship policy that, although on the statute book, has sunk without trace!

Unions and politics

With little or no resistance from their Liberal Democrat junior partners, the Tory Party found it difficult not to use its position in government to attack trade unions.

In response to the exposé of corrupt practices in Parliament (cash for questions) in 2013, the government legislated against trade unions, and other civil society organisations, in the Transparency of Lobbying, Non-Party Campaigning & Trade Union Administration Act that will:

- Limit third party election funding (union support for Labour); and,
- Oblige unions to conduct an annual audit of membership and ensure its accuracy, giving the state powers to access information about union members' private relations with his/her union.

To its credit, the Labour Party has given a commitment to repeal this law if it should win the next General Election.

The Carr Review

In the aftermath of Unite's dispute with Ineos at Grangemouth, the Government announced it was setting up an inquiry, led by Bruce Carr QC (who had acted for British Airways against Unite), into the conduct of industrial disputes.

The Carr Inquiry received no support from trade unions and only patchy support from employers. The terms of reference of the Carr Inquiry were to provide an assessment of both the alleged use of extreme tactics in industrial disputes, including so-called 'leverage' tactics; and the effectiveness of the existing legal framework to prevent inappropriate or intimidatory actions in trade disputes.

In advance of Carr reporting, the Prime Minster announced in May 2014 that new restrictions would be introduced on strikes in 'essential' services if the Conservatives were to win the 2015 general election.

Cameron said he intends to introduce a minimum threshold on the number of employees who must take part in a ballot on industrial action before it can trigger a strike.

Furthermore, Conservative members of the government responded to the public sector strikes held in July 2014 not by seeking a resolution of the issues, but by suggesting that further reform of trade union law was necessary.

The Conservatives said that they would seek to legislate in two areas:

- Creating a threshold for the turnout in an industrial action ballot that must be reached; and

- Placing a time limit on the legality of a mandate a union has to call industrial action.

In August 2014, clearly worried by these pre-emptive policy announcements made by the Conservatives on how they were to legislate against the unions after the next General Election, Bruce Carr threw in the towel:

> "… I have become increasingly concerned about the quantity and breadth of evidence that the Review has been able to obtain from both employers and trade unions … I am also concerned about the ability of the Review to operate in a progressively politicised environment in the run up to the General Election … I have reached the conclusion that it will simply not be possible for the Review to put together a substantial enough body of evidence from which to provide a sound basis for making recommendations for change … the Review will produce a scaled-down report … but will make no recommendations for change."

For the past 30 years, all across the globe, wherever the neoliberal writ has run, trade union and workers' rights have been rolled backed. None more so than in the Mediterranean countries that have been subject to an IMF/ECB/EU "bailout". In Greece, Spain and Portugal, employment law and workers' rights have been changed in similar ways as an integral part of the imposed package of structural adjustment. The UK, however, seems to be the only country that is seeking to make these changes voluntarily.

An incoming government could chose to enhance the role of trade unions for any one of three reasons:

- Trade union rights are human rights;
- Trade union presence creates more just and equal workplaces;

- Trade union led collective bargaining is more redistributive than statutory wage setting and will assist on the road from austerity.

Trade union rights are human rights

On 10 December 1948 the General Assembly of the United Nations adopted and proclaimed the Universal Declaration of Human Rights. Article 23 (4) of the Declaration states that: "Everyone has the right to form and to join trade unions for the protection of his interests".

The International Labour Organization (ILO – a specialist agency of the United Nations that deals with industrial relations and employment issues) published ILO Convention 87 on the Freedom of Association and Protection of the Right to Organise in 1948, which was ratified by the UK on 27 June 1949.

The Convention, which has the standing of an international treaty, states that:

- "Workers ... shall have the right to establish and ... join organisations of their own choosing;'
- Each Member of the ILO for which this Convention is in force undertakes to take all necessary and appropriate measures to ensure that workers ... may exercise freely the right to organise."

ILO Convention 98 on the Right to Organise and Collective Bargaining was published in 1949 and ratified by the UK on 30 June 1950. It says that:

- "Workers shall enjoy adequate protection against acts of anti-union discrimination in respect of their employment;

- Measures appropriate to national conditions shall be taken … for voluntary negotiation between employers … and workers' organisations, with a view to the regulation of terms and conditions of employment by means of collective agreements."

The European Convention for the Protection of Human Rights and Fundamental Freedoms was adopted by the Council of Europe in 1950. Article 11 of the Convention states that:

- "Everyone has the right to freedom of peaceful assembly and to freedom of association with others, including the right to form and to join trade unions for the protection of his interests."

The European Court of Human Rights, established by the Convention, has shown in two cases involving the Turkish Government in 2008 and 2009 that trade union rights are human rights, and that there is indeed an internationally protected right to bargain collectively and to strike. Small wonder that the constant cry from the Conservatives is that the UK should withdraw from its treaty obligations on human rights!

Articles 5 and 6 of the European Social Charter of 1961, ratified by the UK, say very much the same as ILO Conventions 87 and 98 on the right to organise and bargain collectively. Clause 4 of Article 6 explicitly recognises that workers have a right to strike:

- "…with a view to ensuring the effective exercise of the right to bargain collectively, the Parties undertake … and recognise the right of workers …to collective action in cases of conflicts of interest, including the right to strike, subject to obligations that might arise out of collective agreements previously entered into."

Article 28 of the Charter of Fundamental Rights of the European Union 2000 reiterates this point (notwithstanding the protocol negotiated by the UK Government in 2009 against extending the competency of the European Court):

- "Workers ... or their ... organisations, have, in accordance with Union law and national laws and practices, the right to negotiate and conclude collective agreements at appropriate levels and, in cases of conflicts of interest, to take collective action to defend their interests, including strike action."

Trade union presence creates more just and equal workplaces

Trade union values are Labour values, and vice versa:

- Trade unions provide a "voice" at work – when trade unions are absent employers go to great lengths to create an alternative "voice", thousands of pounds are spent on consultative committees, company councils and similar arrangements. Trade unions provide all those "voice" functions and of course are independent of the employer; in a report published in 2010 the authors concluded that in the private sector strong unions can deliver benefits to both employees and employers alike. The evidence indicated that the voice function provided by strong workplace organisation promotes employment relationships which are both more stable and more constructive in the longer term.

- Trade union workplaces are safer workplaces – all the evidence shows that where there are recognised trade unions there are fewer accidents in the workplace and that everyone benefits from safer systems of work.

- Trade union workplaces are more equal workplaces –
  all the evidence shows that where there are recognised
  trade unions there are also procedures that ensure equal
  treatment at work and that women and ethnic minority employees are less likely to suffer discrimination at
  work.

Collective bargaining is redistributive

There is now a mass of research that conclusively shows that
there has been a major shift in income and wealth to the
already wealthy over the past 35 years. Richard Wilkinson and
Kate Picket's ground-breaking work in 'The Spirit Level', plus
the Poverty & Social Exclusion project and work by the Joseph
Rowntree Foundation lead the way in exposing this unwel-
come trend.

To summarise some of these findings:

- Britain is moving backwards towards levels of inequality in wealth and poverty last seen more than 40 years
  ago.

- The general pattern is of increases in social equality
  during the 1970s, followed by rising inequality in the
  1980s and 1990s.

- 'Average' households (neither poor nor wealthy) have
  been diminishing in number and gradually disappear-
  ing from London and the South East.

- Over the last 30 years, Britain has become increasingly
  unequal. The size of the economy has doubled. But the
  fruits of growth have been increasingly captured by
  those on the highest incomes, leaving those on middle
  and low incomes further and further behind.

Only those with a wilful disregard of the evidence, or those who were biased in favour of the rich, could fail to make the link between these findings and the trends described at the beginning of this article.

The neoliberal project, as outlined by Hayek, to smash collective bargaining, to restore to the ruling elite that which was taken from them on the global stage by the New Deal and the post-war victory of social democracy in western Europe, has worked only too well.

The precipitous decline in the coverage of collective bargaining is clearly correlated with diminishing real-term incomes for large numbers of working people, which is more recently compounded by the austerity measures being pursued by the Coalition government.

Any incoming government interested in paths from austerity and in a redistributive society must surely restore to the unions the right and opportunities to bargain collectively on behalf of their members, and to create the conditions where employers are bound to engage in this process.

CHAPTER 12

THE POLITICAL IMPASSE

By Austin Mitchell

Austin Mitchell has been the Member of Parliament for Great Grimsby since 1977

As THE NATION moves towards the next election Labour faces the most difficult policy dilemma that has ever confronted us. In previous elections it was clear what the party of change and reform had to do, in order to remedy the nation's problems and repair the damage done by Conservative predecessors. This was obvious and had widespread popular support. Today there is bitter argument over policies, and even about the nature of the problem. The nation is confused and nervous. The vested interests, most of them against change, are strongly entrenched and have enormous media power to condition the people. Worse still, a sizeable proportion of the electorate is opting out of both politics and the two-party choice which is the only way of securing change in Britain. All this combines to create the possibility that no party will win either a clear majority or a mandate to tackle Britain's problems. We face a political impasse with a third of the electorate Labour, a third Tory and a third so pissed off that they either don't vote or turn to UKIP. A political deadlock and minority governments must be the result.

The basic choice facing Labour and the nation relates to the radical policies appropriate to the scale of the problems of a failing economy which can neither pay the nation's way in the world nor support the employment levels and the social standards an advanced society needs. It can't generate the growth for betterment either. Yet can we deal with this by adopting cautious policies which frighten neither electors nor the dominant vested interests?

On the one hand, we could break the deadlock by re-enthusing the alienated and winning back the four million voters we lost between 1997 and 2010. These voters drifted into alienation or UKIP protest voting because not only did we not deliver enough to them, but because, by endorsing free market economics, globalisation, privatisation and incentive taxation, we helped to destroy their world. They voted for us thinking: "Things can only get better". They didn't. On the contrary, New Labour gave the next Tory government excuses for further follies: "You did it first." Indeed, mostly, we did. On the other hand, we dare not frighten the nation's ever nervous "business" community, shatter confidence abroad and at home or frighten home owners who benefit from price rises which exclude many. Nor do we want to face hostility from a press mostly owned by the wealthy which reflects their *weltanshauung* and interests and sets the terms of debate for the electronic media.

Milder versions of this dilemma were usually resolved in the past by the failure of the incumbent government and "time for a change". This government's failures have been legion, its ideological preoccupations have all been directed at benefiting wealth and punishing the poor, and its austerity doesn't work, can't work and shouldn't be sustained. Yet revival is in the air, not from any long term economic plan (there was only slash and burn), but because any government which keeps interest rates flat to the floor and dumps £375 billion of printed money

into the banks is bound to get some recovery, even if most of
its first four years were wasted. So the race is now between
the pain of memory and the prospects of recovery. It starts
worryingly because Labour in opposition isn't as far ahead as it
should be at this juncture.

So what do we do? We could opt for a respectable caution,
backed by a nice pledge card of bread and butter issues offering
to improve things from utility charges to "bedroom taxes", and
hope to win as the largest single party. That wouldn't confer
a strong mandate but would create the possibility of another
election as in 1964 and 1974. Or we could go radical, by offering a New Deal of regeneration and economic nation building
of the type that built powerful economies for Germany, Japan,
Korea and China, but now comes with the difficulties and
disciplines they faced and prohibitions they didn't.

Such is the choice. It lies between left and right; though of
course in the real world, which practical politicians inhabit,
no one will choose either extreme, lock, stock and barrel.
Pragmatism will suggest a blend. Whichever we choose will be
caricatured and criticised by the media. Nevertheless, in view
of the accumulating problems of a failing economy, my view
is that the stance must be radical. Nothing else can offer hope,
or break out of the deadlock into which the decline in the two
party vote and the inertial power of the vested interests have
locked the nation. If we don't break out, then even tougher
measures will be required to avoid disaster later. Which leaves
one clinching point: should the priorities of a business sector,
which has so manifestly failed, dictate the terms of Labour`s
efforts to reverse the failure?

The answer must be "No". Britain needs a new deal, and Labour
a radical approach. This can be sold to a nervous electorate
on the basis of an appeal to the nationalism latent in every

British breast, which should be central to a party representing those who can't just up and leave, taking their wealth with them. It should also appeal to the British instinct for fairness and equality. Combine these appeals and we have a powerful driving force for a return to the social democratic basics that New Labour diluted. This points to a manifesto that can hardly be set out here but should embrace ten basics.

First. Restore Keynesian economic management. Austerity does not work but makes recession worse by slashing demand; so every person out of work, every drop in demand increases the deficit and requires more borrowing. Only growth can allow debt to be paid off and that turns borrowing, a cardinal crime in Tory eyes, into an essential weapon in a recession. When companies and households are either heavy with debt or reluctant to invest because of prevailing uncertainty, government alone can borrow more and spend the money to generate the Keynesian multiplier. We could hand the dosh out to the people in bonuses, job subsidies and other stimulants. Some have even suggested we could drop the money from helicopters.

The best demonstration of this is the contrast between the US and Europe. In the US, a big stimulus package (which was in fact too small) set the economy back on the road to growth and jobs so that unemployment, which had risen by 5% in the recession, has now fallen by 4%. Compare this with Europe, where Germany insisted on austerity and refused to allow economic stimulus, and so the equivalent 5% rise in their unemployment fell only by 1%. In Britain, borrowing to finance a huge housing programme will slash benefit bills, create jobs, boost demand for household products and stimulate the economy.

Second. We need an industrial policy to build up the powerful exporting sector other nations have developed. This must channel investment, training support, job subsidies, transport, planning and export support to manufacturing, in order to shift the balance of the economy from consumption to production, and from spending to investment. Lacking the national champions of Germany's Mittelstand, Britain must build powerful exporting companies, provide venture capital and channel investment away from the speculative priorities of Finance. A regional policy and regional subsidies can boost the declining areas hit by de-industrialisation.

Third. Markets increase inequality by favouring the rich and powerful at the expense of the poor and vulnerable. We gave too much scope to Finance and to big corporations whose power has increased, is increasing and ought to be diminished. It's time to swing the balance back. We didn't regulate either our privatised industries which boosted profits by ever higher charges or Britain's crony capitalism which pursues profit at any cost. Only the state can regulate and restrain capitalism, which will cheat and chisel unless it's properly controlled. The state is the community in action, and the best, sometimes only, defender of the people. So rebuild the mixed economy by keeping the banks and taking back the railways as contracts fall in. A nationalised railway run as a united entity is less expensive than heavy subsidies and high fares for train operators. Failing companies can be taken over, or protected by a Chapter II bankruptcy provision of the type that saved Chrysler and GM in the US. Why should state enterprise not boost the competition so many sectors need?

Fourth. The rebalancing of the economy from Finance to production requires effective regulation of the Finance sector whose speculative drives caused the crisis. Banks should be split between trading and speculative roles, rather than the ring-fencing the Tories propose. Derivative speculation should be taxed as the gambling it is. Hedge funds, private equity and the huge neo-banking sector must be brought under effective regulation. Encourage longer-term shareholding by taxing early share disposals heavily, and require the funds to monitor the companies they invest in.

A Business Commission should regulate takeovers and ensure effective corporate governance. That means bringing workers onto boards and audit committees, and empowering employees to control top salaries and bonuses. We can break the conspiracy between accountants and managements to hype profits that boost top management pay by banning the sale of services to audit clients and requiring the rotation of auditors.

Britain is too open to foreign takeovers. Because our trade deficit is so heavy we have had to sell companies and allow our economy to be colonised on a scale that no other country permits. This means that the investment decisions of all too much of "British" business are dictated by overseas imperatives, not ours. Time to put up the "End of Sale" sign, make foreign takeovers more difficult, put "national interest" back into takeover legislation and require investment commitments from incomers. Redundancy terms should be raised above Europe's, in order to end the incentive for multinationals to close British production units in contraction because it's cheaper to pay off British workers than French or Dutch.

Fifth. Rebuilding Britain requires a distance from the European Union and its follies. As long as the EU sees "ever closer union" as achievable through the euro, Britain's absence from its "top table" is like the passenger who missed the Titanic. The EU provides a stage for our failed political class to strut on, but it also takes away our power to manage our own immigration, industrial and regional policies and drains money out through excessive contributions. We should use their drive down the dead end Euro Street to extract concessions, including substantial reductions in our contribution, currently £10 billion net, the end of the Common Fisheries Policy to rebuild our fishing industry, and of the CAP which still costs every family £30 a week for Europe's dear food. We should also offer the nation an in/out referendum after a renegotiation. That's only democratic.

Labour became vacuously Euro-enthusiastic because the Party and the unions saw the EU as the source of good things like union and employment rights. We can better provide these by ourselves, had we but the guts to do so. Fear is the only real argument of the euro-enthusiasts, like their claim that three million jobs are under threat, as if Europe would cease to trade with us. That and the fear that we would be alone in the world if we rock the boat are symptoms of an inferiority complex, not statements of reality. So act for ourselves and do what needs to be done. Or leave.

Sixth. Socialism is about growth. It brings altruism, optimism and betterment, but requires sustained competitiveness and cheap money to stimulate investment by the long-term guarantee of profitability which capitalism needs to invest. That means an exchange rate kept low to build a strong, internationally traded sector making continuous improvement by continuous investment. Avoid further house price bubbles by building public housing for rent, and controlling private sector rents, conditions and mortgage lending. Invest in production via a public venture capital fund and the state banks. Finance public projects through public money, pension fund investment and printing by Quantitative Easing finance for public contracts, not expensive PFIs.

Inflation as a target for Bank of England creates a deflationary onus. Replace it by growth and full employment targets and an injunction to put the competitiveness of sterling first.

Seventh. Use the tax system to build fairness and equality. Take tax policy out of the hands of the Big Four accountancy houses by turning their consultants out of their temples and ending HMRC's cosy "relationship building" which allowed Vodafone to avoid £8 billion in interest rate penalties, and the whole sector to escape an estimated £25 billion in tax obligations. Council Tax bandings should be widened and less regressive, with much higher taxes on houses over £1 million in value and a nil band on sheltered housing. Shift the tax system to higher rates on earnings over £200,000 a year, with penal rates on bonuses and share options. Require all profits generated in this country to be taxed in this country.

Eighth. Run the economy and foreign policy for Labour's purposes, not those of wealth or the USA. We are no longer rich enough to afford a role as World Policeman, or even World PCSO. Something's got to give. It should be Defence – where the burden is too heavy and Trident unnecessary – the World role, and all wars which are none of our business. Defence is one area Europe could take on as a collective responsibility. It obstinately refuses to do so.

Ninth. New Labour was lightweight on policy, heavy-handed in management. Tough legislation on terrorism and crime, centralisation, and the concentration of power at the top grew apace. Instead we need to spread power around and transfer it down to local authorities and elected regional governments in, say, six big English regions. Functions should be restored to local government, particularly by bringing Gove's patchwork mass of academies, free schools, company-run schools and community schools back under local authority control so that communities can take pride in education. Similarly, we should give social services a greater role in a health service to be run by publicly accountable bodies, not private contractors.

This democratisation process can also be extended to the private sector by enhancing worker participation, encouraging mutuals, and putting worker representatives on boards, audit and remuneration committees. This will make companies more stable, more concerned with the long term, and committed to investment rather than speculative gains to boost bonuses at the top.

Tenth. Recast the Party by dedicating it to the education of more members and the wider community. Labour is a failing machine, run from the top down and too preoccupied with structures and techniques. We waste our lives in endless committees, while Conference has been emasculated and gives no real influence for the rank and file, who neither feel involved nor inspired by policies which aren't theirs. Recruit more members by a lower membership fee and demand less from them in boring meetings and endless committees. We could have two levels of membership: masochists paying the full rate, the majority -associate members - £5 to put them on a mailing list and send them regular Party information. Party schools and summer camps can give them an influence on and greater knowledge of policies that are far more important than PR.

The easy criticism of this 10-point plan will be that it's a reversion to the past. That is appropriate to a country that has gone backwards because neo-liberalism, market economies and globalisation have undermined the post-war settlement and boosted profit and wealth, not performance or the people. Thatcherite market economics seemed to work only because of world growth, a benign economic environment, and North Sea oil, which was invested in unemployment, not national strength. Labour's basics have all worked before to sustain steady growth, and by returning to those basics (which are still alive in both the Party and the electorate) we can use them to rebuild a strong economy. That requires us neither to trim our sails to every populist and media wind, nor to don hair shirts, but to develop and sell a coherent, socialist alternative to neoliberal follies and back it by mobilising national pride.

Tough times demand tough remedies, not the soft populism New Labour offered in the better circumstances of 1997. Britain is weaker, the economy is failing and under-invested, and unemployment is still far too high. We are not out of recession and have missed four years of vital economic growth. Only boldness can now break out of the political deadlock and only socialist basics can offer a way back, just as they did in the Great Depression and in our post-war recovery. Then, as now, reconstruction was a national as well as a socialist imperative. Then, as now, national regeneration is a national duty with a more effective appeal than diluting everything Labour stands for to prove ourselves respectable to the fiscal powers which caused the recession in the first place. Why are we so timid?

CHAPTER 13
TAX, TAX AVOIDANCE AND TAX EVASION: ISSUES FOR SOCIAL DEMOCRATS

By Richard Murphy

Richard Murphy is a chartered accountant, a social justice campaigner and an advisor to the TUC on taxation and economic issues.

TAX is the lifeblood of any government.

Tax is also fundamental to social-democratic thinking. If social democracy means anything it is that we believe that the government must manage a mixed economy so that, as a result of its interventions, post-tax income and wealth is more equally distributed than pre-tax income and wealth. That makes the tax system in itself a mechanism for achieving Social Democrats' aims. More than that though, without tax, social-democratic governments would not have most of the resources needed to deliver a programme to create a more just society. Well-managed tax systems are, therefore, of particular importance to any debate on the future of social democracy.

The amount of tax that a government collects is based upon a relatively simple formula:

(Tax rate x tax base) - Tax gap = Tax yield

Social Democrats will want a progressive system of tax rates. They will also seek a wide tax base to ensure that as wide a range of economic activity as possible is subject to taxation: firstly to reduce the risk of there being loopholes in the tax system capable of exploitation, and secondly to ensure tax is charged equitably across the population as a whole. Achieving each of these goals is a subject of importance in its own right, but the issue that has come to the forefront of the tax debate in recent years has been the tax gap.

The tax gap is the difference between the amount of tax that should be paid in a given period, if all the laws of a jurisdiction worked as its parliament intended, and the amount of tax that is actually paid. It is made up of three components.

The first - to which least attention is paid - is the tax that is declared to be owed by taxpayers but which they then do not settle on time or at all. As a result of their late or non-payment, the government must borrow to make up the shortfall, as well as dedicating resources to trying to recover the sums due, and sometimes suffering a bad debt. My latest estimate of losses arising for this reason, based on most recent HMRC data, is about £18 billion a year, made up of £5.1 billion of bad debt and £13.1 billion of debt discharged by HM Revenue & Customs in the tax year 2013/14.

The second component of the tax gap is tax evaded. Tax evasion is a criminal activity. It describes the activity under-taken by those who do not declare their income to H M Revenue & Customs, or who claim expenses to offset against their income to which they are not entitled. Of the two, the first is almost certainly the most important. Estimates of the total sum evaded each year vary. H M Revenue & Customs estimate the sum to be approximately £22 billion a year. That would, however, suggest that the UK was the most honest nation on Earth, with less than 5% of all tax lost to evasion each year. I estimate the sum to be about £85bn a year: almost four times that estimated by HMRC. Of this I estimate that approximately £47 billion arises as a result of activity in the shadow economy. This sum, at around 10% of total tax due, is consistent with H M Revenue & Customs as correct of VAT, and in line with estimates for similar European countries made by the World Bank and others.

The third component of the tax gap is tax avoidance. This is the element that most people find hardest to understand. Tax avoidance *is not* the act of claiming the allowances that you are entitled to in law. So, for example, claiming your personal allowances is not tax avoidance. Nor is paying money into a pension fund, or saving in an ISA. Tax avoidance is instead seeking to get around the law so that less tax is paid than Parliament intended on the economic activity that a person undertakes.

This "getting round" the law can be done in a number of ways. Tax avoiders can exploit loopholes in UK tax law, or they can exploit the interrelationship between different accounting conventions and tax law. Most commonly, however, at least in terms of value, tax avoidance involves exploitation of the differences between the UK's tax system and the tax systems of other countries, and in particular those of tax havens.

So, for example, our banks and other UK multinational corporations commonly set up structures offshore to avoid stamp duty, corporation tax and the obligation to pay National Insurance when staff are paid. In addition, the UK's domicile rule turns the UK into a tax haven for the world's mega-rich, creating inequality in our society whilst undermining the tax systems of both the UK and other countries on a systematic basis. More routinely, offshore trusts and companies are used by those with wealth to avoid their obligations to pay inheritance tax and capital gains tax, thus preserving wealth inequalities in the UK.

Any government that is serious about creating a just society has to tackle these issues. Thankfully, just as over the last few years awareness of this issue has risen as a result of the work of a small group of tax campaigners, so have a number of solutions to this problem been proposed. All of these propositions would help close the tax gap and increase equality within the UK tax system, whilst supporting honest business to conduct its operations on a level playing field without the distortions that tax cheats bring into the economy. It is only possible to mention a few of these here.

The biggest misuse of tax havens by large companies involves the abuse of what are called transfer-pricing regulations. Transfer pricing happens whenever two companies under common control trade with each other. This is, of course, commonplace in groups of companies. In that situation, companies are meant to trade at market prices if tax rules are to be complied with. However, there is an obvious incentive to abuse such arrangements to shift profit from high tax locations, such as the UK and most European countries, into low tax locations such as Ireland and the UK's tax havens, including Jersey, Guernsey, the Isle of Man and the Cayman Islands. A new method of accounting for multinational corporations has been proposed to tackle this issue. This is called country-by-country reporting. It would require that the multinational corporation publish a profit and loss account for every location in which they trade. This would then show how much these companies use tax havens, and it would also show how much of that use is purely for the purposes of relocating profits out of the UK and into low tax jurisdictions. This may not stop transfer mispricing directly, but the simple exposure of profit-shifting activity in their accounts would force a change in behaviour by these companies, and so help stop their international tax avoidance. The OECD has now endorsed this methodology for use for this precise purpose; what is also needed is that the data that multinational corporations will now have to create for tax authorities be put on public record. The impact of public pressure can then be brought to bear on these companies to stop this abuse, which is currently facilitated by the veil of secrecy that tax havens provide to them.

The second obvious way to tackle tax avoidance would be to abolish the UK's domicile rule. No other countries – apart from Ireland, and Italy to a limited extent – have such a rule which lets people of foreign origin who are resident in their country be exempt from all tax on their worldwide income, except that arising there. It is commonplace everywhere else that a person resident in a country pays tax on their worldwide income. The UK should follow this example, and stop letting the UK be used by the world's mega-rich as their favourite tax haven. This behaviour on their part increases divisions in UK society, probably contravenes the UK's equality laws, and definitely creates injustice in our tax system whilst encouraging abuse by those who cannot avail themselves of this rule.

Another mechanism for tackling tax avoidance would be for a comprehensive general anti-avoidance principle to be incorporated in United Kingdom law. The current government has introduced a very weak version of such a provision, but amongst its many faults HMRC actually require the effective consent of a panel of representatives of the tax profession, before they can use it against the abuse that that profession has created. What is needed is a much more robust and principles-based anti-avoidance measure that says that if a taxpayer puts steps into a transaction for the sole reason of seeking to reduce their tax bill then that step will be ignored when it comes to assessing their tax. This shifts the entire balance of power in tax avoidance towards the government and away from the tax abuser. Both the European Union and Organisation for Economic Cooperation and Development are now supporting such measures. It is overdue that the UK adopted a mechanism that can deliver on the promise that the recently created law we have is clearly incapable of supplying.

Finally, steps must be mentioned that tackle tax evasion, because this is an enormous issue. As my research has shown, one way of tackling this enormous issue is to spend considerably more money regulating private limited companies that operate in the United Kingdom. Extraordinarily, with about 3.2 million such companies existing in 2014, around 400,000 of them are dissolved each year without any demands being made on them to pay any tax that they might owe. In most cases they were dissolved because all contact with them had been lost by regulatory authorities. In addition around 600,000 companies are not asked to submit tax returns by HMRC in most years, and of those that are asked to make returns hundreds of thousands do not actually do so, and hundreds of thousands more declare that they have no income, with very few checks appearing to be made on these companies by HMRC. As a result, of all the companies that exist in the UK in the last year for which data is available, only about 1.1 million actually paid tax.

Of course, and inevitably, some of those companies that failed to file returns did no doubt make a loss; even so it is highly likely, in my estimate, that more than 400,000 companies that are trading in the UK in each year do not submit tax returns, and because of the shortage of resources available to both HM

Revenue & Customs and the Registrar of Companies, no action is taken to recover any of the tax owed by these companies. I estimate that these companies alone might result in a tax loss to the UK economy of at least £12 billion a year, and maybe more. Yet what is significant is that this abuse indicates that a lack of investment in resources for HMRC means that tax losses are being incurred that could otherwise be avoided. The tax gap is, in other words, optional whilst tax evasion in the small business economy is tolerated, and the balance between honest and dishonest traders has been tilted heavily in favour of those willing to commit crime.

The case for tackling tax avoidance and tax evasion is compelling. Alongside measures to create progressive taxation, resourcing our tax authority so that it can deliver tax justice is an essential component of Social Democratic economic policy.

CHAPTER 14

BUILDING THE FOUNDATIONS OF
A MORE EQUAL SOCIETY

By Richard Wilkinson and Kate Pickett

Richard Wilkinson and Kate Pickett are the authors of 'The Spirit Level: Why More Equal Societies Almost Always Do Better'

IN THE 1960s levels of income inequality in Sweden and the UK were quite similar. But the gap between the richest and poorest 20% in the UK is now twice as big as in Sweden and other Scandinavian countries. Much the most rapid increase in inequality in the UK happened during the 1980s.

We start this essay with a brief summary of the evidence which shows how damaging such large income differences are for the wellbeing of the vast majority of the population – not just to the poor. We then go on to suggest ways of making the necessary very substantial reductions in income differences. These include ways of making greater equality more deeply rooted in our society so that gains are less easily reversed.

The social cost of inequality

A wide range of social problems tend to be more common lower down the social hierarchy. Problems such as ill health, violence, teenage birth rates, lower levels of child wellbeing, low maths and literacy scores, are all more common in the more deprived areas and among people lower on the social ladder. It is easy to imagine that this pattern is caused simply by a tendency for social mobility to move the vulnerable down the social ladder while the resilient climb to the top.

However, internationally comparable data shows that these problems are between twice as common and ten times as common in societies with bigger income differences between rich and poor. No process of sorting people through social mobility would, of itself, make any characteristic more common in the population as a whole: it would only change where people rank in society. So even if it is partly true that social mobility tends to separate the resilient from the vulnerable, that cannot explain why more unequal societies have much greater burdens of ill health and social problems. The fact that they do means that these problems are substantially responses to social status differentiation itself. It suggests that a very large proportion of the problems with social gradients are actually *caused* by social status differentiation itself.

What the data show is very simple: problems which are related to social status within our societies get worse when social status differences increase. The bigger the income differences, the more important social status differences become. Larger economic and material differences between us increase the *social distances* between us, making society more class-ridden. And whether income differences are larger or smaller determines whether the whole social class pyramid in society is taller and steeper or broader and flatter.

The vast majority of the population, across all political parties, think that social class differences and their effects on us should be reduced. Well-meaning statements are sometimes made to this effect by Prime Ministers from the front door of 10 Downing Street as they take office after an election victory. But it is essential to remember that anyone who really wants to reduce social class differences in society must reduce the income differences on which they depend.

The differences in the prevalence of health and social problems between more and less equal societies are large. In 'The Spirit Level' we showed close to ten-fold differences in teenage birth rates and in the proportion of the population in prison. Other studies have shown equally large differences in homicide rates related to inequality. Using WHO figures we found three-fold differences in rates of mental illness and two-fold differences in infant mortality. These differences are so large because it is not just the poor who are affected by inequality. Studies which allow us to compare people in more equal societies with their counterparts at the same level in the social hierarchy in less equal societies, show that the benefits of greater equality extend to the vast majority of the population. Although we do not have separate figures on health, teenage births and violence among the fraction of one per cent of the population who are the super-rich, the data does allow us to say with some confidence that 90 or 95% of the population benefit from living in a more equal society.

What that means is that given a person's position in the job hierarchy, or their particular level of income or education, if that person lived at the same level in a more equal society, they would be likely to live a little longer and be less likely to become a victim of violence. Their children might do a little better at school and would be less likely to get involved with drugs or become teenage parents. We illustrated this important point using data from five peer-reviewed studies. In a sixth, colleagues at the Harvard School of Public Health went as far as to say that inequality acted as a "general social pollutant" because its damaging effects extended so far up the income scale. In each case, people lower down the social hierarchy benefited most from greater equality but, to a lesser extent, even those near the top benefited.

The reasons why the effects of inequality extend so far up the social scale are not hard to understand. First, although the problems affected by inequality are most common at the bottom of the social ladder, they also occur at the top. Problems such as ill-health, depression, violence and drug abuse occur at all levels in society – they just become more common further down. Indeed, health inequalities run right across the society: instead of being a difference in health between the poor and everyone else, health improves at every step up the social hierarchy. To understand health inequalities it is not enough to think only about unemployment and homelessness. They account for only a very small part of health inequalities. We also need to explain why very comfortably off people with good incomes and education, secure jobs and homes, have less good health than those even better off above them.

Although the causal pathways vary for each health and social problem, a key to all of them is the effect which inequality has on the nature of social relations in societies. By increasing status differences greater inequality increases status competition and status insecurity. The data from a number of different studies show how inequality weakens community life and makes people feel less likely to trust each other. People in more unequal societies have less contact with each other; they become less cooperative and more out for themselves. As status becomes more important, we judge each other's worth more by status and, as a result, feel more worried about how we are seen and judged. Inevitably, money becomes more important because we use it to show our worth to others. Consequently people in more unequal societies are more consumerist: they work longer hours, spend more of their income, save less, and are more likely to get into debt.

Because we become more insecure about how we are seen and judged, social relations in society at large become more stressful. Social contact is only relaxed among friends. Elsewhere it can become an ordeal and increasingly we need the privacy of our own homes to relax. Levels of what psychologists have called the "social evaluative threat" are raised. Studies of stress hormones show that they rise not just with any kind of stress, but particularly when we are worried about how we appear to others, when we feel others might judge us negatively, when our self-esteem or social status is at stake. And of course these concerns go all the way up the social hierarchy. This has social and biological consequences for all of us.

An important part of the general sense that the political left lost its sense of direction was a loss of confidence in its long term commitment to greater equality. That was mainly because people thought about the effects on inequality from an almost exclusively material standpoint. In the 1930s, when so many people were living in great squalor and hardship, it was obviously wrong for others to be living in great luxury. But now that the vast majority of the British population have central heating, DVD players, fridge-freezers and cars, many people began to wonder if inequality still mattered. What we failed to see was that some of the most important effects of inequality are psychosocial. Almost all the outcomes we looked at in 'The Spirit Level' (including violence, drugs, teenage births, maths and literacy scores, social mobility, social cohesion) are behavioural outcomes reflecting the psychosocial effects of inequality. Instead of reflecting the direct effects of inadequate material circumstances themselves, they testify to the powerful social processes set in train by emphasising social rank, hierarchy and people's sense of superiority and inferiority, of being valued and devalued. This is why inequality has to be reduced whatever the level of overall wealth.

Reducing income differences

So what should be done to reduce income differences? Some countries gain their greater equality by redistributing income through taxes and benefits, but others do so through smaller differences in income before tax. As judged by the levels of health and social problems in a society, what really seems to matter is the level of inequality you end up with – not how you got there. But if the UK is to achieve the levels of inequality found in the more equal of the rich developed market democracies, we would need to halve inequality. That is not something which can be achieved with a few short term tweaks to top tax rates or by providing slightly more generous benefits. Interestingly, although almost all Gordon Brown's budgets redistributed from rich to poor, the effects on inequality were more than offset by rapid increases in the pre-tax incomes of the rich.

Before governments can return top tax rates to anything like the levels they reached in the USA and Britain in the 1960s and '70s, tax havens will have to be brought under control. But we need to reduce income differences before tax as well as redistribute through taxes and benefits. Too much reliance on taxes and benefits is a weakness because any new government can change taxes and benefits at the stroke of a pen. We need to find more fundamental ways of making our society more equal.

The main reason why income differences widened so much in Britain and many other countries over the last generation is that top incomes have run away from the rest of us. Much the fastest increase in inequality came in the 1980s and that coincided with legislation which weakened trade unions. Several studies have shown that more equal countries tend to have strong trade union movements.

The bonus culture and the vastly inflated top salaries seem to reflect a total lack of effective democratic accountability at the top: it looks as if those at the top thought they could do whatever they liked. Income ratios between CEOs of the FTSE100 companies and the lowest paid full time workers in the same company are typically about 300:1. The proper response to this is to increase democratic accountability within companies – everything from requiring that there are trade union or employee representatives on company boards, to increasing the number of employee owned and controlled companies. In general, companies with more democratic structures – whether mutuals, friendly societies, producer and consumer cooperatives or employee owned companies – have much smaller income differences within them. As consumers we should move our custom to these kinds of companies and governments should set up loan funds and provide tax incentives to help employee buyouts.

To achieve a really substantial reduction in inequality we will need a campaign committed to that objective lasting for perhaps a decade or two. Over such a long time period we have to think how that would combine with another essential long term objective: the need to make dramatic reductions in carbon emissions to deal with global warming and to develop a sustainable way of life. An important reason why politicians have been slow to address either task is because both are thought to require unpopular belt-tightening policies.

Reducing inequality often seems to be a matter of whether the middle class would tolerate an increase in taxes to spend on the poor. Similarly, reducing carbon emissions is often thought of in terms of imposing green taxes and curtailing consumption.

We need to turn the tables on these pessimistic views and create an inspiring vision of the kind of society we should be moving towards. After all, the reason why people in the past committed themselves to the socialist cause was not because they thought that problems could be solved with a few minor policy adjustments. They did so because they thought a better world was possible for all of us. We know what went wrong with that project; we now need a new vision of where our societies should be going and of the kind of world we should be moving towards. And if it is to be sufficiently inspiring to gain people's commitment, it must be a view of a world which will make life qualitatively better for all of us.

Some of the most important elements of the kind of society we should be moving towards are already clear. By extending democracy into our economic institutions and workplaces, we not only lay the foundations for a more enduringly egalitarian society and raise everyone's psychosocial wellbeing while doing so, but we would also transform the experience of work. Employee ownership can change a company from being a piece of property into a community. We complain that we have lost community in residential neighbourhoods and decry the fact that people no longer know their neighbours, but it is at work that we interact most with each other. But the potential for a strong sense of community at work is damaged because it is also at work that inequality is created by income differences and reinforced by hierarchy and line management. With something more like a community at work, the work place might more often provide people with a sense of self-worth, of being valued by colleagues and of making a contribution.

Evaluations of more democratic companies suggest that combining employee ownership with participative management produces reliable improvements in productivity. However, an important reason why this sector of the economy has not grown faster is because employees are often tempted to sell their shareholding back to external shareholders. Constitutions should be drawn up to remove this temptation. To accelerate the growth of this sector of the economy, governments need to establish funds to help employee buyouts. Loans would be repaid from trading profits and reused to support further buy outs. Tax incentives would also help to increase the proportion of these kinds of company in the national economy.

As well as narrowing income differences and providing a new basis for community, there are two other advantages in expanding the cooperative and employee owned sector of the economy. First, employees would be very unlikely to vote for their company and jobs to be transferred to countries with cheaper labour. Second, if work became a place where people felt they were valued and their contribution appreciated – rather than simply feeling used and exploited, there would presumably be less reason to fear either that people would abuse sick leave or that less punitive unemployment benefits would make people 'work-shy'.

Greater equality also has an important contribution to make towards the achievement of sustainability. The greatest obstacle to achieving sustainability is consumerism. But consumerism is very substantially about status competition which is, in turn, amplified by inequality. As we noted earlier, money becomes even more important in more unequal societies because we use consumption to show our status and worth. The implication is that if we are to reduce consumerism, we must reduce inequality.

Another important link between greater equality and sustainability is that more equal societies appear to be more public-spirited. This reflects the fact that community life is stronger in these societies and people are more likely to trust each other. Rather than people feeling that life is basically about having to fend for themselves, there seems to be a greater concern for the common good. More equal countries give a higher proportion of their national income in development aid. They score better on the Global Peace Index and surveys show that business leaders in more equal countries think that environmental issues are more important than do their counterparts in more unequal countries. More equal countries also recycle more of their waste materials and produce less carbon per $1,000 of National Income.

It is possible then to begin to sketch a picture of the kind of society we should be moving towards: a society in which reductions in inequality have improved the real quality of our lives, in which the experience of work has been transformed, in which democracy has been extended into the economic sphere, and in which we are very much nearer achieving environmental sustainability. The task of progressive governments is to embed greater equality into the structure of society.

CHAPTER 15

AFTER OZYMANDIAS:
WILL LABOUR MISS
THE ENERGY REVOLUTION?

By Alan Simpson

Alan Simpson was the Member of Parliament for Nottingham South from 1992 to 2010.

.... Two vast and trunkless legs of stone

Stand in the desert. Near them, on the sand,

Half sunk, a shattered visage lies, whose frown,

And wrinkled lip, and sneer of cold command,

Tell that its sculptor well those passions read!

Which yet survive, stamped on these lifeless things ...

IN ENERGY POLICY, the next Labour government will inherit two 'vast and trunkless legs of stone' from the Coalition. These are its obsessions with fossil fuels and nuclear power. For another generation, both obsessions could condemn Labour to the pursuit of 'lifeless things'; missing the energy revolution already taking place around us.

It doesn't have to be like this. This should be a bumper time for Labour.

The Coalition's energy and climate policies are a feast of all that is incompetent, regressive, or both. From the debacle of Green Deal to the suicide tryst with 'Freedom to Frack'; from its pandering to a greedy and self-serving (Big 6) energy cartel, to the ludicrously expensive subsidies to new nuclear; from the repeated kickings given to renewable energy to the raft of new allowances for old oil; Labour is being presented with a set of open goals that even the England team would struggle to miss. Yet this is precisely what the Party could do.

Today's energy revolution is not being defined by individual technologies: it is rooted in how we think about energy systems as a whole. To understand the extent to which Labour fails to grasp this – and the scale of its potential policy misjudgments – it may be easier to start from a non-technical example.

As a child, the red telephone box seemed to me to be a benchmark of civilisation. I depended on the availability of phone boxes to call home if I was going to be late, to ring for a taxi when I'd missed the last bus, or to phone my mates (when I didn't want the whole family listening in). In those days, the landline was the lifeline.

Not any more. Today's iPad generation knows that you don't have to haul telephone boxes or mainframe computers around with you to communicate with the world outside. Technologies that deliver 10 times more, using 10 times less energy, are a given in modern life. The whole world is now at your fingertips or in your pocket. This is what will happen to tomorrow's energy systems.

An obsession with building big power stations will be seen as little more than 20th century penis politics. Only sad people will find security there.

Tomorrow's world

Tomorrow's energy systems will not be designed around old style power stations. They may not revolve around power stations at all.

Big Energy knows this, and is terrified. Within a decade, half of today's energy corporations will have gone bust. Without huge public subsidies, financial markets will no longer underwrite them. Without unsustainable dividends, investors won't put their money into them. Energy systems will become both more decentralised and more interconnected. The energy we don't use (and the energy we store) will become at least as important as the energy we consume. Energy security will be found, and financed, in a myriad of different ways.

Anyone even glancing towards tomorrow knows that its energy systems will be smarter, quicker, lighter, more adaptive and more interactive than anything we have today. Only a bunch of idiots would saddle Britain with an energy investment programme obsessed with the past rather than the future; and at a cost that will sink the country rather than save it. Yet this is precisely what the Coalition government will have done.

The Coalition of confusion

The Energy Act 2013 is probably the worst piece of energy legislation in my lifetime. Obsessed with the past, it would continue to put 'dirty' energy before 'clean'. Instead of a more open and democratic energy market, it seeks to prop up a dysfunctional cartel. Instead of an emphasis on markets that sell 'less', it remains wedded to ones that consume more. Written by Big Energy, it will entrench the power of Big Energy.

The Energy Act 2013 will come to symbolise the debacle that is this Coalition government. Climate change deniers are now at the helm of the Tory Party. Their influence runs from the oil obsessions of the Chancellor and the BIS, to unfathomable DECC commitments to 'Contracts for Difference' and 'Capacity Payments'.

Lib-Dem MPs, who remember that they once had coherent energy policies, openly weep about a Secretary of State who could barely negotiate an unconditional surrender. His 'tough negotiations' with the nuclear industry – offering an index-linked, 35-year price guarantee that is three times the cost of today's 'new nuclear' in Finland – make Britain a laughing stock across Europe.

Elsewhere, renewable energy technologies plough ahead on ever-falling cost curves. Yet the Energy Act 2013 will squeeze both sustainability and democracy out of the UK's energy market. Britain's Coalition of climate deniers and out-to-lunchers have pledged the country to yesterday's most unsustainable energy sources, at tomorrow's most unaffordable prices!!

It is a debacle that cries out for a good kicking.

A different vision?

For a moment, Labour looked to have grasped this. Ed Miliband's conference pledge of a 20 month price freeze sent expectations soaring about bigger plans to radically transform the energy market. In the silences that followed, such expectations came crashing to earth. Those looking for anything transformational soon gave up holding their breath.

The most unkind rumours were that Labour's price freeze had been no more than a last minute inclusion in Ed's speech.

More worrying were suggestions that, in the week following, Ed's office was so panicked by the onslaught from Big Energy – threatening to kill off all UK energy infrastructure investment until the freeze ended – that they immediately pledged to stand by all the most stupid energy policies adopted by the Coalition.

So it was that Labour's Energy Green Paper found itself trapped in a 'Coalition-Lite' approach to energy policy thinking.

Ed Davey's Energy Act 2013 may be an extraordinarily dumb piece of legislation, but dumber still would be a Labour pledge to stand by it. Under the guise of 'stability', many of its most useless elements would then emerge as Labour commitments too.

The curse of 'lifeless things'

How easy it is to envisage Labour opting for everything deceptively safe and sterile. Instead of a radical commitment to transform the future, Labour could fall for the seedier charms of 'cold command' of the past; propping up an existing cartel of Britain's non-renewable energy interests.

Everything unsustainable could find itself being endorsed – a quiet furtle with fracking; a bit of nookie with nukes; a mild flirtation with fuel poverty; a dalliance (but no more) with decentralisation; but only a fluttering of eyelids towards new social ownership models of energy systems that use less, but deliver more.

This is the crossroads at which we stand. In a world that must learn to use less fossil fuel, the Coalition has thrown financial rewards into extracting more. In an era where the renewable will overtake the non-renewable, the UK has prioritised the opposite. In a future driven by energy technologies that are lighter, smarter and (increasingly) cheaper than today's lumbering power stations, Britain remains wedded to an outdated past.

Of course, Labour could try to blame it all on George Osborne, but the truth is more complicated. Labour remains equally gripped by a Treasury mindset that fails to understand the real crisis we face; that tomorrow's economics will either be 'Green' economics or no economics at all.

What the world faces is a paradigm shift, not a cyclical crisis. Bailing out the banks only made it worse, because governments nationalised gambling debt at the expense of financing environmental repair and infrastructure renewal.

Look back in anguish

The legacy of binge-borrowing and binge-spending is just the first (and perhaps easiest) of the challenges a Labour government will have to face. Forty years ago the Club of Rome (in their 'Limits to Growth' report) set out strategies needed to avoid drifting into a much bigger global environmental crisis. The world took little notice, and raced off in the wrong direction.

Their follow-up analysis – '2052' – is even more stark. The planet faces huge (and rising) bills for the climate damage we have already caused. There are even bigger bills for the damage we might yet avoid. With the melting of the West Antarctic ice cap already past its tipping point, large parts of tomorrow's economics will be about damage limitation and repair.

Skip the debate between climate deniers and climate scientists.
Cut to the insurance industry's annual figures on environmental damage costs. For them, floods, droughts, hurricanes and
storms are now part of the *regular* 'extreme' weather events we
must live with. It will get worse.

Liberalised economies risk becoming polarised between the
unemployable and the uninsurable. Socialised solutions will
become the only workable solutions. But tomorrow's solutions
will have to be forged in an era yet to rediscover that the collective has become more important than the individual. It will not
be an easy journey back.

A better quality of 'less'?

The industrial world is set to become poorer over the next 40
years. GDP growth will be low to non-existent. Countries will
not be able to shop their way out of successive climate crises.
An increasing proportion of GDP will go into environmental
investment and repair. 'Growth', if it has a meaning, will have
to become a quality of life index rather than a quantity of
consumption.

Yet it is within this maelstrom that Labour could yet take
Britain into the astonishing world of opportunities and transformation that lies beyond: a world in which we learn to live
more lightly, creatively, and interdependently.

Resuscitating the past is a waste of time and (public) money.
The problem is not just a dependence on old technologies, but
the clapped-out mindset that forms the basis of UK Treasury
thinking. The question for Labour is whether it can break up the
Treasury before the Treasury breaks the Labour government?

New ideas, new ground rules

Collective security will be the unifying theme of all the major challenges ahead. The cornerstones of **democracy, openness and accountability** will have to connect to the question of (meaningful) common stewardship of resources.

In terms of energy policy, this is not about old style re-nationalisation of the Grid or of energy companies. It is more about a policy framework that will socialise the production and distribution of energy (in a sustainable context) at the same time as delivering markets that consume less. This is also an invitation to grasp what the shift from an energy oligarchy to an energy democracy might look like; defining a new 'politics beyond the power station'; and setting new ground rules for energy markets that sell local (and even non-) consumption.

These are questions that still frighten Labour. It is too easily panicked by the 'lights might go out' scare stories used to prop up the current subsidy system. Labour has lost confidence in its ability to offer a more exciting narrative that could inspire the public about a more secure future.

Tomorrow's homes and workplaces will increasingly purchase energy *services* rather than energy supply. Much of the energy will be produced on-site, pooled or stored. Grid balancing will come (transnationally) from interconnectors and (locally) from demand management. New power stations will become, at best, a secondary consideration. Engineering and innovation skills will be drawn to the management of dynamic grids rather than baseload power. It is the world Labour could yet lead Britain into.

Privately, energy companies already see this writing on the wall. Their historic neglect of infrastructure investment is combining with the falling cost of renewables to make even the attractions of going off-grid (or local grid) increasingly plausible. You can already see this in parts of the USA.

In the first quarter of 2013, over 80% of new energy installed in the US was renewable energy. The rest was gas. This was a blip, but alarm bells were already ringing. In January 2013, the Edison Electric Institute – an entrenched voice of 'old energy' – published its own warning that renewable/decentralised energy was about to change everything. Its report, *'Disruptive Challenges: Financial Implications and Strategic Responses to a Changing Retail Electric Business'*, saw the industry writing its own obituary: "The financial implications of these [renewable/ decentralised energy] threats are fairly evident. Start with the increased cost of supporting a network capable of managing and integrating distributed generation sources. Next, under most rate structures, add the decline in revenues attributed to revenues lost from sales foregone. These forces lead to increased revenues required from remaining customers … and sought through rate increases. The result of higher electricity prices and competitive threats will encourage a higher rate of [decentralised energy] additions, or will promote greater use of efficiency or demand-side solutions.

Increased uncertainty and risk will not be welcomed by investors, who will seek a higher return on investment and force defensive-minded investors to reduce exposure to the sector. These competitive and financial risks would likely erode credit quality. The decline in credit quality will lead to a higher cost of capital, putting further pressure on customer rates. Ultimately, capital availability will be reduced, and this will affect future investment plans. The cycle of decline has been previously witnessed in technology-disrupted sectors (such as telecommunications) and other deregulated industries (airlines)."

They could have just written, "Game over".

In plain English, Edison issued a warning that new energy infrastructures will make it possible for the public to walk away from old ones. The cost of propping up the past will become increasingly prohibitive. Old empires (and profit streams) are about to go down the pan.

An industry that has not seen its structure change in a hundred years is suddenly staring down the barrel of extinction. Only in Britain are these realities held in suspended animation by a political class that just doesn't get out enough.

News from elsewhere

Fortunately, many other countries are already well on the way into tomorrow's energy thinking.

Denmark led the way, after the 1973 oil crisis, by ensuring that all of its new building would be based around district heating networks. Today, you cannot get planning permission for a new building that uses fossil fuel heating. By 2050 the Danish economy will be based on 100% use of renewable energy. Not far behind will come Germany (80% by 2050), Austria (34% by 2020, and maybe more than Germany by 2050), the Scandinavian countries, Italy and Spain.

As a 'one country' example it is worth looking at Germany. In the last seven years, the country has moved from an energy sector dominated by their 'Big 4' power companies, to one in which there are almost 2 million new energy suppliers. Germany now has an installed capacity of over 70GW of renewable electricity (about the same as the UK's peak demand). And it's still growing.

All this is part of their *Energiewende* (Energy Transformation) programme: a market transformation that will radically cut carbon emissions, boost energy security, create jobs and grow the economy.

In 2012, only 5% of the new German generating capacity was owned by energy companies. The majority belonged to households, communities, farmers and businesses. Towns, cities and villages not only generate much of their own energy, they are also taking local distribution networks into the public domain; using community rights to 'buy back' the energy they generate (at wholesale rather than retail prices) as a way of cutting consumer energy bills.

In September, 2013, citizens in Berlin 'won and lost' a referendum on whether to take the Berlin Grid into social ownership. Whilst 83% of voters said 'yes', the turnout failed to cross the threshold that made it binding. They will be back.

What matters, in the context of Britain's energy debate, is not the outcome of this referendum, but the presumption that German citizens have an *entitlement* to make such choices.

Any 'One Nation Britain' will have to incorporate the same approach to citizens rights in the UK, if it is to step beyond the window dressing politics of the last decade.

Changes in the ownership of the German energy sector have also unleashed a wave of technology innovation. Central to this was a recognition that today's key energy partners are more likely to come from the technology and communications sectors than from the power sector.

Myth busters

Thankfully, the Germans have also broken two of the Treasury/ Tory press myths deployed against 'green economics'; firstly, is that it is an economic burden rather than a blessing; and secondly, that it is only affordable *after* a crisis not in the middle of one.

In an era where most industrial nations have seen GDP fall, Germany managed to grow its economy *and* to shrink its carbon emissions. This was no accident.

The next table demonstrates the correlation between energy transformation and per capita GDP.

Far from being an unaffordable cost, the German Environment Ministry estimates that, in 2010 alone, renewable energy reduced their cost of energy imports by **€6.7billion.**

Moreover, **this part of the German transformation programme required no government subsidy.**

- German citizens (and businesses) invest **€30 billion of their own money each year** in renewable energy schemes

- The FITs (Feed-in-Tariffs) system pays people for the 'clean' electricity they generate.

- It exists as a free-standing element within German energy sector accounting.

- *FITs* are not a public subsidy and *do not count against public expenditure limits.*

- Renewable energy has to be taken first by the Grid; forcing German peak power prices to fall to their lowest levels in the last five years; and

- It has delivered over *380,000 new jobs* in the same period.

Germany expects that, in meeting its 2020 target (of 40% carbon reductions), their *Energiewende* programme will also deliver:

- €22bn savings in 'avoided' fuel imports per year;

- An annual increase of over €20bn in GDP; and

- A profit of €0.34 cents on every tonne of carbon saved.

By 2030, the net effect will make their national debt **€180bn** lower than if there had been no climate protection measures. Such energy economics are the antidote to a crisis, not an afterthought to it.

Lighter, brighter, more dynamic and democratic: this is the shape of tomorrow's energy systems. The tragedy is that, in Britain, you cannot even get the Treasury to do the same maths let alone the same journey.

Not here, please – we're British

When Rainer Baake, former permanent secretary in the German Environment Department, came to the House of Commons last year, he was asked where a British *Energiewende* should start from. His answer was simple. "Don't get hung up on technologies. Britain's problem is that it has no *vision* of what tomorrow's energy systems will look like". It is a truth that is painful for Labour to embrace.

Britain led the world in the last two energy revolutions but is seriously adrift from the current one. Elsewhere, nations, localities and even energy companies themselves are waking up to the emergence of a very different energy landscape. Democracy drives this as much as sustainability.

Over 190 German localities are taking their local energy grids back into social ownership. Central to this is the right of German citizens to the 'first use' of the energy they generate, buying locally at *wholesale* rather than retail prices. This has triggered a huge wave of investment and innovation in smart technologies to share, store and manage energy flows. It offers Germans the prospect of cutting energy bills at the same time as cutting carbon emissions. When has Britain's rigged energy market offered such a choice to UK households?

By bringing local distribution grids back into the public domain, cities and regions (as well as smaller towns and villages) are begining to socialise their energy security. Insulating homes, schools, offices and businesses becomes part of tomorrow's low energy agenda. It also turns out to be a lot cheaper than building new power stations ... and it delivers lots more jobs.

Britain may struggle to give meaning to its platitudes about support for 'community energy', but elsewhere there is nothing like the same reticence. Many of the new institutions that German energy networks revolve around are commonly owned. They currently have over 600 energy co-operatives. Britain struggles to maintain 50 that are viable.

Mutuality is the safe road back to interdependency. The variability of renewable energy flows are currently proving easier to address through inter-connection than storage. This may change as technology advances, but inter-regional interdependencies will take us into new meanings of common security.

For the UK, this may be via the current European energy grid, or extensions of it to Norway, Ireland and even Iceland. The key is to treat these as *strategic national assets* rather than as trading investments. Future energy security will need to be judged by the strength of the safety net, not by its return on investment. This is where the state, rather than the market, must step in.

After Ozymandias

Tomorrow's economics are more likely to revolve around the **localisation of security** than the globalisation of trade. Countries will find their own ways around WTO rules and the deregulatory delusions of the last few decades. It isn't difficult. Big business does it all the time. And, in the face of global summits delivering less and less, bilateral agreements will see the mutual interests of states displacing the transient interests of corporations.

The era of a global free-for-all led mainstream political parties to create a rod for their own backs. Each competed for the same political space, chasing the same sweetheart deals with transnational business and footloose capital. While rights and freedoms were transferred to corporations, citizens were left with burdens and responsibilities. When the bubble burst only the debts and disillusionment remained.

Today's legacy is an accumulation of public contempt that gets drawn towards protest voting, or not voting at all. Politically, tomorrow's credible space will have to create genuinely open, accountable and sustainable energy markets that the public have some faith in. Like it or not, each political party will have to stumble towards an engagement with these new realities.

As they do so, political parties will also discover it is a cheaper route towards energy security. The €30bn Germans annually invest in renewable energy comes at interest rates of less than 6% p.a. For the public, this is a lot better than leaving it in the bank, but for energy companies it falls a long way short of the 12% they expect before getting out of bed.

In Germany, it was Angela Merkel's centre-right who recognised that *Energiewende* is allowing them to be both popular and frugal at the same time. In the UK, whoever wakes up to this reality first will steal the ground from other parties. As the SPD is now discovering in Germany, it is hard to reclaim progressive space once someone else has occupied it.

At the moment, however, the British public are offered little more than an array of false and foolish choices:

- Throwing huge subsidies at the one technology on a spiralling cost curve which delivers no new energy within a decade (nuclear);

- Endorsing a panic-driven extension of the most polluting power plants (coal) without the precondition of 100% carbon capture; or

- Heavily financing a dash for shale gas, even though the industry knows it cannot get the technology to work in Europe.

These are not solutions, just props to a system already past its 'sell by' date.

What Labour must do

An incoming Labour government, committed to the Coalition policies it inherited, would be on a suicide mission, with policies that are as unaffordable as they are unworkable. The immediate crises in the middle of this decade will require a more radical refocusing of priorities and resources.

A fifth of UK electricity generating power will be about to go off-line. The fear of a **capacity crunch** will be used by the press (and Old Energy) to panic Labour into pledging huge subsidies to the past. Where market support is needed, **Labour must**

**pledge that public subsidies will go to a sustainable future,
not an unsustainable past.** It would be no bad time for Labour
to open up a wider debate about how far such public subsidies
should come in the form of public stakeholdings rather than
corporate handouts. This would scare the socks off the Tories.

Beyond this, Labour needs its own set of visionary
commitments.

1) **Energy efficiency.** This could be Labour's economic,
   energy and environmental *el Dorado*. Energy efficiency
   programmes deliver savings (and jobs) far more rapidly
   than new power generation or even new construction:

   - *Taking half a million households a year out of fuel
     poverty* would give people something to vote for, well
     beyond the delusions of the Green Deal. This could be
     done by initially turning the Warm Zones pilot schemes
     into a national programme, and channelling all ECO
     funding through them; and

   - *Giving local authorities the power to purchase and
     upgrade vacant properties for social housing purposes*
     – and borrowing (at 1%) via the Green Investment Bank
     would transform the housing renewal programme.

2) **Decentralised (community owned) renewable energy
   generation** would make the public 'partners' in Labour's
   task of *Empowering Britain*. Labour should commit to:

   - *Giving priority Grid access to renewables.* 'Taking
     clean energy before dirty' will be the hallmark of tomor-
     row's energy thinking. Countries within the EU already
     have the right to apply such a 'Merit Order Effect' to
     the operation of their Grid systems. In Britain, the dead
     hand of Ofgem, Old Energy and climate denialism has

blocked every attempt to follow suit. It is an obstruction Labour could sweep away.

- *Local power markets.* Labour must pioneer markets where people can pool the energy they generate, *without incurring full Grid Access and balancing charges.* These would make the public part of the solution, not just those who pay for the problems.

- *Local grids.* Even if conventional energy prices continue to rise, energy bills do not have to. Storage, balancing and sharing technologies will be the cornerstone of tomorrow's energy thinking. This is one of the most exciting ways in which Labour could deliver a more open, dynamic (and affordable) energy market.

This would put Labour on the side of the small millions rather than the Big 6.

3) **Tomorrow's Grid: markets that sell less.** Future energy distribution systems will sell energy savings as much as energy consumption (and local generation). Labour needs to socialise the Grid, following the lead of countries with a stronger tradition of decentralised governance. It is doubtful that UK could do so in one step. As a starting point, however, **local authorities (or Local Economic Partnerships)** could be given the power to:

a) Act as the local monitoring body that holds the DNO to account for the delivery of national targets for carbon reduction, renewable energy and demand reduction; and

b) Set higher local targets, should they so decide.

The effect of this would be to make the public key players in the determining their own (appropriate) local energy security policies.

4) **Avoiding the capacity crunch: obligation and interconnection.** Public fears about 'the lights going out' will be used to box Labour into a costly and ineffective policy space. Energy companies are already preparing to 'game' the system, pocketing new subsidies for old answers. Labour has to have ready answers to the (artificial) crisis. These should include:

- **Regulatory Reserve Requirements,** similar to those in banking, but which require all major power generators to hold a 10% capacity reserve; and

- **Building new interconnectors as a part of a UK strategic reserve,** allowing the UK to benefit from current (low cost) surpluses in the European Grid and offering a market for UK's surpluses.

A real future for the kids

What the Coalition wants to avoid (at all costs) is the prospect of an incoming Labour government committed to any profound 'systems change' to the UK energy market. In reality, this is the only thing Labour *should* commit to.

We live in a world that has to learn how to leave carbon where it is; where public (or environmental) wellbeing has to displace today's corporate welfare state. The future rests in the hands of those who will rediscover how we dance with nature rather than stomp all over it.

The coming General Election offers a moment crying out for visionaries rather than functionaries. And when you get beyond the drivel of media imagery and spin, this is the one quality Ed Miliband could bring to the Party. He just needs to reach past the over-cautious, short-termist, playground politics of the Party he inherited and define a better politics of tomorrow.

No secure future will be found by parties obsessed with yesterday's telephone boxes. The world has moved on. Politics must too.

The landline is no longer the lifeline.

CHAPTER 16

HOUSING: THE BIG BUILD

By Austin Mitchell

Austin *Mitchell has been the Member of Parliament for Great Grimsby since 1977*

HIGH QUALITY, affordable housing for all is basic to the good society. It's also the policy field in which Labour's last government failed the most. Good health requires good housing, eliminating crowded, damp, dirty conditions and the stresses and insecurities of deprivation. Good education needs continuity for kids in school and good home conditions that give them space to work, read and think. Safe neighbourhoods need settled, stable, mixed communities, not ghettos where the poor take their miseries out on each other. Yet Britain's slow progress towards these goals has been undermined over the last four decades. The old social compact whereby Britain's low wages were compensated by cheap food and cheap council housing has gone. Eighteen years of Tory disinvestment privatised much of the stock, pushed up prices and led to a housing crisis. Labour failed to repair the damage because its build rate was low for private housing, lower for social housing and pathetic for council housing. Need grew as households multiplied, but the build rate fell lower than any decade since

185

the 1920s – only 112,630 completions in 2013–14. An incoming Labour government will therefore face a crisis with growing homelessness, rising prices at the highest ever ratio to stagnant incomes leaving a rising proportion of the people unable to buy, and a higher proportion of purchasers living with negative equity which they can't afford if interest rates rise.

This happened because New Labour, anxious to minimise spending commitments, concentrated everything on health and education. So little money was left for housing, despite the huge job to be done after 18 years of Tory disinvestment and the sell-off of over two million council houses. Estates had been allowed to deteriorate, building up a repair and renovation bill estimated at £19bn. Labour couldn't pay that and opted instead for accelerated privatisation: bullying, bribing and bamboo-zling councils into handing over billions of pounds worth of the public housing which they had built up to provide for their people, to housing associations who raised their money on the private market. Government preached the virtues of owner-ship, even though many Labour voters could hardly afford it, and encouraged it by an array of schemes and grants, including help for key workers and rental purchase schemes. All of this added fuel to the flames of the ever rising prices produced by scarcity.

The inevitable result was a mess: galloping house prices, soar-ing private rents, rising waiting lists and a growing housing shortage. Prices rose to the highest multiple of earnings ever, putting ownership out of reach for between a third and a half of the population, depending whether they lived in the North or the South. The stock of council housing shrank to a record low of 2.5 million units because of privatisation and the continuation of Right to Buy: up to a third of houses bought under Right to Buy were sold on to the private rental sector. Conditions deteriorated on all too many estates as scarcity turned them from mixed communities into dumping grounds where only those in desperate need had any chance of priority. The commendable effort to bring social and council housing up to the Decent Homes Standard by 2010 lagged so badly that it won't be completed until 2015, and too often depended on privatisation.

As the 2010 election approached, the long campaign waged by the defenders of council housing finally succeeded in changing government policies, because government needed to stimulate the economy after the 2007–08 recession. The result was more money, a restart to council house building, "kick start" help to rescue stalled building schemes, help for those threatened with repossession, and new proposals to stop Treasury's theft of around £1.6bn a year, and all the funds from Right to Buy sales from Housing Revenue Accounts, something the Party Conference had demanded for four years running. The build rate for social housing went up from 14,000 to 26,000, including council houses.

Too little, too late because the Tories won the election, immediately reversed the gains and made a bad situation worse. Capital funding for social housing was halved. The housing associations were encouraged to make up the difference by raising rents to a less affordable 80% of market rates. This, coupled with the cuts in housing benefit in 2012, was part of a process of turning the limited stock of council and social housing into an overpriced transit camp, by scrapping secure tenancies and introducing both fixed-term tenancies and means testing to force out tenants who improved their lot or earned too much. Then came the "bedroom tax" to evict those who didn't make use of all their space. Supposedly all this is to make room for those in greater need, but the overall result has been to destabilise council and social housing, shrink the stock and turn both into ghettos of poverty and exclusion, far from the mixed communities Labour once set out to build. Declining ghettos, too, as the Right to Buy reductions reached give-away levels and the government failed to deliver its promise of building a replacement for every house sold.

At the same time the process of pushing rents up to the levels of the private sector began. In that rapidly growing sector, government obstinately refused to interfere or regulate to prevent overcrowding and an emerging new Rachmanism, as unscrupulous buy-to-rent landlords bought cheap housing (often repossessed council houses), many of them sight unseen at auction, and shoved any tenants they could get in them to claim housing benefit while the landlord waited for the house prices to rise.

The inevitable result is a compounding housing crisis which the next Labour government will have to deal with. That means giving housing a much higher priority and committing to give all households access to secure, affordable, good quality housing in sustainable communities. This will require a massive house-building programme on a scale clearly indicated by the widening gap between need and delivery. Labour's target of building 200,000 a year by 2020 is modest by both the scale of the problem and our performance of the past

The Barker Report in 2004 estimated that the number of households would grow from 20.9 million to 25.7 million by 2026, or 209,000 a year. Some of this growth will come from a multiplication of single-person householders, the rest from immigration and population growth. The estimate was raised to 232,000 a year by the National Statistics department in 2008. Yet actual delivery has hovered just over 100,000 a year, and though both parties envisaged increasing it, both failed to make any real progress towards this goal. Delivery fell under the Tories. There is huge ground to be made up to allow Labour to achieve its basic task of housing the people.

Like Caesar's Gaul the housing problem comes in three parts: private home ownership; the heavily subsidised private rented sector, which has grown rapidly in recent years; and the shrinking proportion of public housing for rent. This isn't to be confused with "affordable housing" which is much talked of but rarely affordable, since it really means "slightly less unaffordable". The proportion of the housing stock which is owned (67%) has fallen slightly since 2007 because of rising prices but is substantially bigger than in France and Germany (which suffered less from the house price bubble as a result) and lower than in Spain and Ireland (where the bubble was worse). It is not likely to change much, though the Tory Help to Buy scheme is pushing prices up by boosting demand, not supply.

An incoming government must achieve a better balance between the two, for while making it more difficult for more and more of the English to own their castles, ever rising prices have drawn too much of the nation's investment flow into housing and away from more productive uses. Better balance can be achieved by boosting supply with a bigger build, while rationing demand by limiting mortgages to 80% of valuation. It can also be achieved by making the most expensive houses less attractive: by trebling stamp duty on houses over £2m; making Council Tax less regressive by adding more high bands; and adding a Mansion Tax on the very biggest houses.

The private rented sector is at its highest proportion ever. 1.3 million families with children live in it, and the number of households in the sector increased by 600,000 between 2009–10 and 2012–13. By encouraging people and businesses to buy to rent government has driven ever more finance into housing, at the cost of enormously increasing the housing benefit bill, so much of which has gone into subsidising the higher rents charged by private landlords. Rather than letting this go on, the best way of rebalancing the market is by building more public housing for rent as a cheaper alternative and by increasing the responsibilities of the landlord and the security of tenure in the private sector. There will always be a market for upmarket rentals for business transfers, well-off tenants and middle-class transients, but unchecked growth at lower levels has brought in what can only be described as cheap jack, even slum landlords, buying cheap housing to make a quick gain on a rising market. This has led to a decline in standards, maintenance and care, as poor tenants have been put in to be financed by housing benefit. This new Rachmanism needs firm regulations, rent control and provision for greater security and length of tenure, with stronger powers to councils to take over housing where the landlords do not fulfil their responsibilities or provide proper standards.

The greatest need is also the area that has seen the greatest failure: public housing for rent, whether social housing provided by housing associations or council housing. The Thatcher revolution was most damaging to housing in this area, for Right to Buy drastically reduced the stock - and is still reducing it, picking huge holes in the estates. Both processes were continued apace by New Labour as council stock was transferred to housing associations. Sale might have been acceptable if a new council house had been built for every one sold under the even better terms the Tories allowed, but that promise was not fulfilled. The build rate fell drastically under both governments and, amazingly, the money for new social housing was cut by 60%. The result is a paradoxical situation. Britain needs a far bigger stock of public housing for rent, to provide housing for that huge and growing proportion of the population who are never going to be able to buy or even raise the deposit, with the average house price £285,000, according to the Office of

National Statistics, and £499,000 in London. To achieve that, young buyers on a salary of £21,200 would need a mortgage nine times their income. According to the Halifax average prices have risen by £17,261 in the last year alone, while average earnings went up only 0.6%. They're still rising. Tories know that pleases home owners.

Incredibly, no-one talks of more council housing or social housing but only of affordable houses. These are private houses created under Clause 106 agreements between builders who agree to build a proportion of cheaper houses in their estates in return for planning permission to build at all. No public money is involved here. The real issue of building public housing at public expense is largely taboo because public housing costs money, which adds to borrowing, and this is public enemy number one for both parties. This must be tackled head on. Borrowing is no crime. Indeed it is a virtue when spending the money stimulates the economy, as building houses did when it drove the recovery from the Great Depression in the Thirties. It also provides a public asset from which councils will derive revenue. Public borrowing is much cheaper than all the private borrowing mortgagees are forced into, and public housing cheaper and better run than privately rented accommodation. So Labour must borrow and build: either through national government borrowing or using housing bonds issued by local councils and guaranteed by the Treasury, paying government's borrowing rates rather than the higher level of interest payable on the market or in PFIs. It's also possible to follow Manchester's example and finance builders out of pension funds on council-owned plots. Finally government can also print money through diverting Quantitative Easing – £375 billion of which has been stuffed into the bank - to finance housing contracts and new town developments with proper terms and pay off. This creates a public asset and would be much cheaper and far better than just giving the money to the banks to build their reserves.

Housing Revenue Accounts should be the council's money to use for housing purposes, not a Treasury milch cow. Councils that retain their stock or want to build new stock should be given full control of their Housing Revenue Accounts, with none of the Treasury subventions currently taken out nominally to pay off an historic debt which has, in fact, already been paid several times over. Add to this the revenue from Right to Buy sales (which would still go on, just not at the cheap discount level offered by the Tories) currently taken by the Treasury. This revenue should also be used to build more houses, always subject to the provisos, which the Tories have ignored, of one new build for every sale and no sale of the new housing built from 2015 until after five years of residence. This will give the local authorities adequate funding to renovate and maintain their stock and a revenue stream on which to borrow more, all backed by an expanding housing stock regenerated and updated as the revenue flows in. On this basis the growing estates could become the mixed communities which they were always intended to be, rather than the dumping grounds for the poor they have been turned into.

To allow this, big-build planning restraints will have to be eased so as not to stand in the way of necessary development. Labour tried compulsion with regional spatial plans and a requirement on local authorities to build and provide land. The Tories, motivated by southern NIMBYism, have removed the compulsions and the regional spatial plans but kept the obligation on local authorities to provide land. The best way forward should be to provide incentives to local authorities to build, by allowing them to keep the rents of all council houses built with no such return on permission to build for private sale. All the incentives should go to a better social mix.

Building can be the responsibility of both associations and councils. Where councils have retained the stock, either directly or through Arm's Length Management Organisations, the new build, like the repair and renovation of the existing stock, will be the responsibility of the local authority, which should also be empowered to check repossessions and bring vacant properties into the public sector. Where housing associations have taken over the stock they can still be brought back under the aegis of the council acting as housing authority for the area. Councils have a better overview of the needs of the area and are more concerned to build to fulfil them, while the associations have proved more enthusiastic about building reserves and balances than houses. They could be municipalised to run the local housing stock as council's agents under the democratic supervision and control of the council. As Not for Profit organisations, this return to the municipal fold is straightforward, and the lower interest rates paid on municipal lending will be an incentive. Where associations have merged or taken over other associations to build sprawling giants without local roots, these bigger entities must either demerge to return to local associations or compete in each area with either a local authority resuming its housing functions, or a new local association building the local stock.

New build and stock improvement are no justification for the higher rents the Conservatives want to impose. Their aim is to put rents up towards market levels. This is an artificial concept, given the scarcity factor which currently makes private rents in most of the country artificially high. Councils should be free to set rents geared to local housing need, which will make them lower than the rents charged by the private sector which reflect scarcity. Unlike the private sector, public sector rents should not be a profit making business but a social service, benefiting from lower council and interest costs in construction, maintenance and management. Tenants should get the benefit and it should not be used as a source of revenue for the Treasury.

Local housing revenues should go to local housing, not be used as a form of taxation of the tenants who live in it.

Whether public housing stock is run directly by the local authority or by a local housing association it must be run with the co-operation and involvement of the tenants. Local authorities were developing better consultation, and housing associations laid emphasis on it, but it tended to wither on the vine since they took over and financial imperatives became more dominant. There must be no return to the bureaucratic and unsympathetic "paint 'em all green" attitude of authoritarian council landlordism. Councils have much to learn from the incentive schemes, the gold tenancies guaranteeing fast repairs, and the local involvement and points-based transfer schemes developed by several associations in the first flush of enthusiasm. The lessons should be learned because this is community housing and the involvement of tenants in the management and running of their own housing is essential.

Housing will be a crucial responsibility for the next Labour government. Labour must plan for it now by committing to a huge housing programme and remedying the failures and inadequacies of our last government. The housing drive will stimulate and boost the economy in a way nothing else can. It will put construction workers back to work, stimulate demand for the furniture and fittings every house needs, and generate the revenues for local and national treasuries. The great housing drive which began in 1932 boosted Britain out of the Great Depression before rearmament took over that process. Labour's new drive can do the same for the Great Recession, the effects of which still linger. It is more necessary than ever. A price fall is desirable for better balance, but an abrupt one would be electorally disastrous. A further rise is even more damaging, would and drain ever more investment out of productive use. Thus a huge build of public housing for rent is the only way to ease out of this trap.

More and better housing will represent a huge advance in social justice. Good housing is not a speculative asset or a gift to the rich but a basic right of everyone, not just of those who can afford to pay today's inflated prices. Council and social housing have developed a ghetto image in the years of housing failure, and dumping grounds are the indicators of a divided society. Expansion, renovation and improvement must take us back to more mixed communities, and provide decent homes to that large proportion of our people who can't afford to buy even the meanest of properties, all of whom deserve the best society can give them. We must help them to bring up their families and to live a life more satisfactory and fulfilling than anything they can get in today's overcrowded, unhealthy and insecure conditions. Housing is basic and our people deserve the best. The next Labour government must provide it. All our efforts in health and education will be vitiated without good housing.

CHAPTER 17

GREEN ECONOMY

By Caroline Lucas

Caroline Lucas is a British Green Party of England and Wales politician who has been the Member of Parliament for Brighton Pavilion since 2010, and is the UK's first ever Green MP.

> *Once there were two children. Tweedledum was the elder and always had the larger slice of cake at tea. Tweedledee, though younger, always demanded an equal share. So their parents, anxious to avoid squabbles, baked a cake that was ever so slightly larger each day. That way, Tweedledee's slice could keep getting bigger, and Tweedledum could still have the larger portion, and after a while, peace reigned. But the children were so used to eating more and more cake that they became enormously fat. And eventually the cake became so big that it was difficult for the family to afford. When they were forced to bake a smaller cake, both children would scream at their parents as well at each other. And so everyone in the family lived in misery ever after.*

IF THIS FABLE sounds familiar, it is because we have all lived through it. Since the 1950s, the western economies have been able to expand production of goods and services to such an extent that the concerns that dominated the 1930s – equality and security – could be pushed to the margins. Expanding production meant that everyone's standard of living could rise, and so the tensions between the haves-mores and the have-lesses were reduced. Progressive taxes were more acceptable to the rich if they could at the same time keep getting richer. And the wish of those nearer the bottom to improve their lot was met by material gain, if not greater equality.

So for decades Left and Right could agree on one thing: that however national income should be divided up and spent, it was better to have more income in the first place. Increasing Gross Domestic Product became the ultimate measure of economic success to which all other policies and targets have to be subjugated.

This came at a price. As the economist J K Galbraith argued as early as the 1950s, chasing GDP growth distorts the economy and has many perverse outcomes. GDP does not distinguish between the production of unnecessary goods and services and those that really matter to people, so an increase in gambling or the sale of luxury yachts is just as good as increases in housing or social care. It also tends to favour private production and consumption over the provision of public goods and services, leading to Galbraith's 'private wealth and public squalor'. Perhaps most insidiously, an economy that constantly pushes for the highest possible levels of growth will be prone to 'boom and bust', so making people's lives far less secure because of inflation, unemployment and volatile interest rates.

By the 1970s, it was also clear that growth was limited by the ability of the planet to provide raw materials and absorb the pollution from economic activity. Economic growth in the West relied on cheap resources and labour in the Third World, and in degrading the natural world at an alarming speed. Even before the oil crisis of 1973 and the instability that followed brought new insecurity and inequality, economists had moved beyond Galbraith's analysis to include environmental and resource issues and map out a 'post-materialist' or 'post-consumerist' world in which improving the quality of people's lives, including promoting equality and security, and not the economy's headline output, was the prime objective. But even as growth of the national cake faltered, both Labour and Conservatives responded with a renewed emphasis on economic expansion.

To achieve this, the Conservatives undermined equality and security through mass unemployment, deregulation, attacks on unions and welfare reform. From 1997, Labour responded by pursuing, a pro-business and pro-growth agenda. Despite the rhetoric traded between the two parties, these governments maintained a consensus that growth, not equality or security, was their prime objective.

Even the wake-up call of the financial crisis has not shattered the consensus amongst the nation's political and business elites. Through Cameron-Osborne's approach is more hard-edged than that of Milliband's-Balls, the assumptions are the same: that policy should aim to 'get the economy moving' at all costs, even if this means accepting higher inflation, greater inequality, cuts in public services, higher unemployment, more pollution, or a more regressive tax regime in which the worst off pay more.

This, then, is the agenda for the 'greening' of the economy. The current consensus is based on economic growth. but we have already reached the limits of what a single planet can sustain, and our standard of living is now dependent on our taking far more than our fair share from poorer countries and from future generations. And despite this, our own country is blighted by inequality and economic and social insecurity. It is no wonder that as a nation we seem to be no happier than we were ten or thirty years ago. Materially, many of us are better off. But in an era of turbo consumerism and aggressive individualism, we have lost our sense of cohesion and seen parts of our public realm increasingly impoverished. The pursuit of GDP growth has only postponed the time when fundamental issues of equality in Britain must be addressed. Though many working people have gained from years of growth, power remains as concentrated in the hands of the few, and the prosperity of individuals and whole communities remains at the whim of the unelected and the unaccountable.

In days gone by, industry used to produce waste and pollution and then use 'end of pipe' solutions to deal with the problem. In recent years, attention has switched to re-designing industrial processes to be more efficient and reduce or even eliminate the pollution in the first place. If we are genuinely to green the economy and so benefit both people and the environment, we need to do the same. The traditional GDP growth model simply causes too much harm to people's lives and to the fabric of our society. It also cannot continue in the face of dwindling, resources and accelerating climate change. But if we can unite to reject the false god of GDP in favour of a new shared goal – a commitment to equality and security throughout society – then we can turn that environmental imperative into a potent agent for social and economic renewal.

www.ingramcontent.com/pod-product-compliance
Lightning Source LLC
Chambersburg PA
CBHW070803280326
41934CB00012B/3043